Fully Visualized

Branding Stories

GINGKO PRESS

Fully Visualized
Branding Stories

First Published in the USA and in Europe in 2019 by

GINGKO PRESS

Gingko Press, Inc.
2332 Fourth Street Suite E
Berkeley, CA 94710 USA
Tel: (510) 898 1195
Fax: (510) 898 1196
Email: books@gingkopress.com
www.gingkopress.com

Gingko Press Verlags GmbH
Schulterblatt 58
D-20357 Hamburg / Germany
Tel: +49 (0)40-291425
Fax: +49 (0)40-291055
Email: gingkopress@t-online.de

ISBN 978-1-58423-704-4

Gingko Press by arrangement with
Sandu Publishing Co., Ltd.

First published in 2019 by Sandu Publishing

Sponsored by Design 360°–
Concept & Design Magazine

Edited and produced by
Sandu Publishing Co., Ltd.

Publisher: Sandu Publishing Co., Ltd.
Chief Editor: Wang Shaoqiang
Executive Editor: Ye Zijun
Copy Editor: Jason Buchholz
Design Director: Wang Shaoqiang
Designers: Huang Zhiyi, Chow Pakwah, Su Zhenhua
Sales Managers: Niu Guanghui (China), Winnie Feng (International)

Graphics on front cover by Serious Studio, Tyodi Hyojin Lee, Ico Design, MONOTYPO Studio, Diferente, Yuan Wang, Xfacta, Menta Picante, Kinda Ghannoum, Hue Studio
Projects on back cover by Diferente, Plus X, Oscar Bastidas, GM Creative Studio
Cover Design by Huang Zhiyi

info@sandupublishing.com
sales@sandupublishing.com
www.sandupublishing.com

Printed and bound in China

CONTENTS

PREFACE

The Image in Brands

"To be is to be perceived" is translated from the famous phrase in Latin: *Esse est percipi*. It is perceived as a conclusion of the leitmotif of the philosophy of Parmenides of Elea, a pre-Socratic Greek philosopher, and is further elucidated by George Berkeley, an Irish philosopher, in his theory of Immaterialism. Berkeley held the view that there are no mind-independent material things. This idea stayed in my head from the first moment I heard it because it reminds me of the fact that I apply my perception to understand the things around me. For example, we get an image from the reality of the collective mind, but usually, we have no idea how far that image can be replicated.

This image can fly through others' minds, at any time, in any place. It stays in one's memory and is replicated in the forms of new images, and thus, that is how we can measure the persistent history of the human race. These images are the meticulous records of life.

So what is the image? Is it just a label to classify groups of objects? What does the image inform us? I think that the more we explore its form, the more we can give it the specific content. It is the principle that moved me and led me to be a graphic designer.

Although graphic design is the solution of a visual problem, it begins as an exercise in understanding the environment. For example, in the search for our origin, it has helped us decipher the keys left by our ancestors, since the images that the archaeologists studied contain the key to our history and legacy, as solving a riddle to decipher, which exactly represents such chimeras. Understanding the images also helps us understand our position in the space and time of the cosmos because we are who we are today, and who we could be.

As graphic designers, we have a natural or even animal attraction to the aesthetic values of an image. We explore the possibilities of building new images and translating feelings, knowledge, history, and the ways of thinking about mere symbols.

Although we began to "interpret" the image from our very experience of life, it is not until we understand the environment that we begin to understand the value of the image as a narrator of the history of an individual—his or her thoughts and legacy.

The identity of the brands that we use daily also tells part of this story. Without a doubt, our exposure to them makes our relationship with them somehow go beyond merely "having a bottle of soda" or "wearing a pair of sports shoes" because our interaction with them represents a part of what we feel and how we think. At this point, the work of the designer transcends beyond pure functionalism. Somehow we hope that our daily life is more joyful and spontaneous with a good design.

As identity designers, we must understand that our work is to extend the horizons of the brand's personality. Our primary tool to approach our work is undoubtedly an anthropological understanding of man, commonly known as archetypes, and the result of such knowledge is manifested in the relationships between our clients and their customers, those who find affinity in what they consume and make it a part of their identity, or tags—for instance: Los Angeles Dodgers fans, Uber users, Barbie doll collectors.

Then the image becomes the very evidence of our existence. As humans, we like to transfigure reality and tell it in different ways, since the image portrayed shows only the surface. To go deeper, to better represent our thoughts, we need to decorate reality—putting flowers on a notebook to make our lives happy, hanging a painting at home—to make us feel inspired when life seems to get boring or repetitive.

If we look back upon the 1960s, we will see many designers who make more than images. Alexander Girard challenged Modernism, a movement that rejects any form of decoration, and put happy faces on his textiles, his furniture, and his objects to express the joy of living. Girard loved life, and he traveled throughout the world, filling his head with inspiration and knowledge. It was important for him to leave his mark on the earth using his graphic. Saul Bass found the bridge between the cinematographic dynamism and the iconicity of graphic design. His work reveals that the image that moves can tell stories and that when we look at an object, we only remember fragments of it. That is why it is easier to remember silhouettes than complete figures. Mirko Illic turned the image into a weapon against the oppression of freedom of expression. I keep in mind his hardest side to give strong hits of reality to the spectator. And Chip Kidd uses the image to make us smarter, more cultured, and open-minded.

The image continues to sell because it refers to the daily history of man. An image that tells us how men collected water from a well 3,000 years ago now can become an image showing us that man can buy bottled water almost anywhere. An image brought from the frescoes of Renaissance paintings that were supposed to invite us to heaven can become the image on digital billboards advertising elegant perfumes. It is our responsibility as designers to continue this record of humanity. What would have been brought to Campbell's canned soup if its identity had been just a can with a white label with generic letters? Had Andy Warhol not painted the iconic image for this brand, what would have happened? Is not the image of *The Last Supper* a souvenir sold outside the Vatican? Would Obama have succeeded in the election without the famous Shepard Fairey poster?

Orlando Portillo
Art Director at Estudio Yeyé

"As identity designers, we must understand that our work is to extend the horizons of the brand's personality. Our primary tool to approach our work is undoubtedly an anthropological understanding of man, commonly known as archetypes, and the result of such knowledge is manifested in the relationships between our clients and their customers, those who find affinity in what they consume and make it a part of their identity, or tags—for instance: Los Angeles Dodgers fans, Uber users, Barbie doll collectors."

Tetrapod

Design Agency • **Plus X**
Creative Direction • **Byun Sabum, Shin Myungsup**
Design • **Kim Hyunwoo, Lee Jihye, Kim Chulhee**

Tetrapod Brewing Co. is a brand that was created by designers, developers and entrepreneurs who love beer. It aims to create an environment where people can bring their stories and spend a great time. Plus X's goal was to differentiate Tetrapod from other pub brands. The name "Tetrapod" comes from the tetrahedral concrete structures used as armor on breakwaters. The core value of the brand is derived from the formative characteristics of these tetrapod and is reflected in the brand design essence through its colors, typography, patterns, and icons. Plus X used recycled papers to convey the rawness of concrete and to reduce environmental impact. To enhance the uniqueness of the identity, they designed various types of products such as cups, sampler trays, coasters, and tap handles.

LOGO

TETRAPOD
BREWING CO.

FONT · Tetrapod Stencil

ABCDEFGHIJKLMN
OPQRSTUVWXYZ
0123456789
~!@#$%^&*()_+=-
“ ”:;,.<>`?/[]\|

COLOR

C0 M80 Y100 K0
C0 M0 Y0 K95
C0 M0 Y0 K0
C0 M0 Y0 K35

GRAPHIC

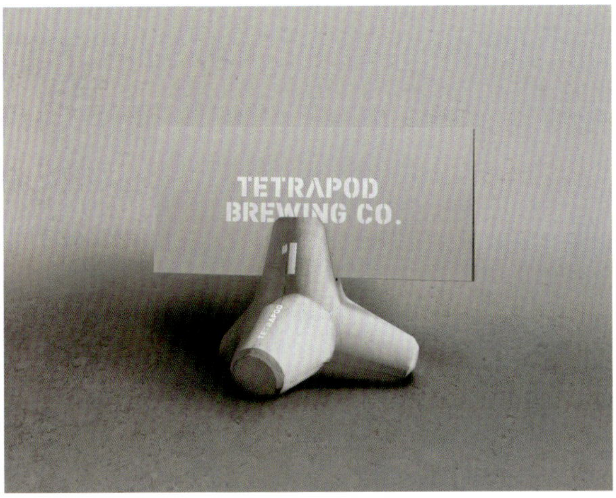
TETRAPOD
BREWING CO.

BRING
YOUR OWN LIFE
TETRAPOD BREWING CO.
BRING
YOUR OWN LIFE
Pale Ale
TETRAPOD BREWING CO.
BRING
YOUR OWN LIFE
TETRAPOD BREWING CO.

TETRAPOD
BREWING CO.
TETRAPOD
BREWING CO.

02
PORTMAN
STOUT
5.0% ABV
TETRAPOD
NEW
BEER
TETRAPOD BREWING CO.
01
TETRAPOD
PALE ALE
4.9% ABV
TETRAPOD
SIGNATURE
BEER
TETRAPOD BREWING CO.
03
TETRAPOD
I.P.A
6.2% ABV
TETRAPOD
POPULAR
BEER
TETRAPOD BREWING CO.

TETRAPOD BREWING CO.
BEER
TETRAPOD PALE ALE
APPETIZER
SMOKE CHICKEN

WE CAN
RELAX YOUR
ROUGH WAVE
TO TETRAPOD
BREWING CO

TETRAPOD BREWING CO.

TETRAPOD BREWING CO.
TETRAPOD PALE ALE
AMERICAN PALE ALE
TETRAPOD BREWING CO.
TETRAPOD BREWING CO.
알코올 함량 및 용량 : 4.9%, 355ml
유통기한 : 제조일로부터 12개월
19세 미만 청소년 판매금지

TETRAPOD
BREWING CO.

Volcano Tourism in Chile

Art Direction • **Asya Demidova**
Design • **Asya Demidova**
Client • **Team Trip**

In order to attract young tourists and draw their attention to volcano tourism in Chile, Asya Demidova created an original tool called "Volcano Passport." With a map, this passport turned usual tourism into a quest game in which every tourist gets a mission to complete. There are 137 stamps, corresponding to Chile's 137 volcanoes, divided into two types—one for people who visit and one for adventure-seekers who climb to the summits. Demidova used minimalistic illustrations instead of photos, which are often used for tourism branding to avoid visual spoilers.

LOGO

VOLCANO TOURISM IN CHILE
MZ ERA
RING OF FIRE ADVENTURE

FONT • Ikaros-light / Kankin

A B C D E F G H I J K L M
N O P Q R S T U V W X Y Z
a b c d e f g h i j k l m
n o p q r s t u v w x y z
1234567890

COLOR

C0 M80 Y100 K0
C0 M0 Y0 K100
C0 M0 Y0 K0

GRAPHIC

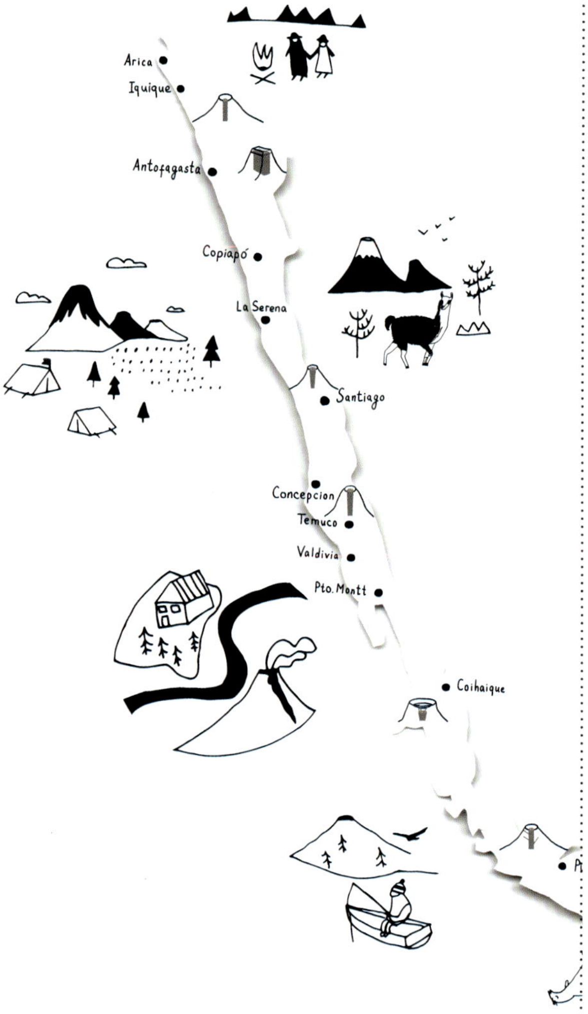

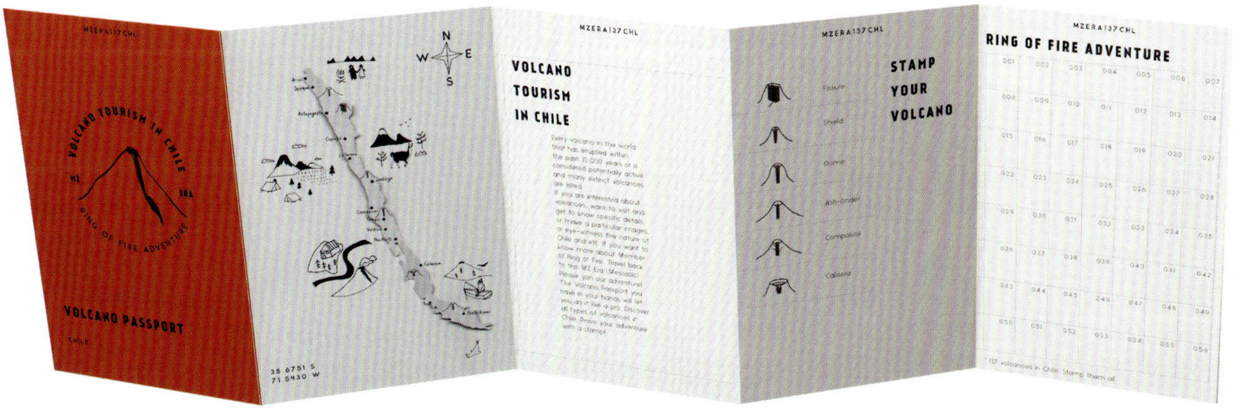
MZERA137CHL
VOLCANO TOURISM IN CHILE
MZ
ERA
RING OF FIRE ADVENTURE
VOLCANO PASSPORT
CHILE
N
W
E
S
35 6751 S
71.5430 W
VOLCANO
TOURISM
IN CHILE
STAMP
YOUR
VOLCANO
Fissure
Shield
Dome
Ash-cinder
Composite
Caldera
RING OF FIRE ADVENTURE

VOLCANO TOURISM IN CHILE
MZ
ERA
RING OF FIRE ADVENTURE
STAMP
YOUR
VOLCANO

VOLCANO TOURISM IN CHILE
MZ
ERA
RING OF FIRE ADVENTURE

RING OF FIRE ADVENTURE

MZERA137CHL

RING OF FIRE ADVENTURE

Tropical Deli Café

Design Agency • **Project On Museum**
Art Direction • **Jay Guan-Jie Peng**
Design • **Jay Guan-Jie Peng**
Client • **Tropical Deli Café, Chan Shuo**
Photography • **Tropical Deli Café, Chan Shuo**

Tropical Deli Café is a multi-functional space located on the first floor of the Museum of National Taipei University of Education. For this project, Project On Museum created an organic, fern-leaf shaped logo and elaborated it into more basic elements. With a combination of those elements and different colors, they created sixteen intriguing plant images and applied them to different items in the store. These basic elements can still be combined and recreated into new plant images, mimicking the mysterious ecosystem of real tropical forests, where numerous new species wait to be discovered.

LOGO

熱 帶
TROPICAL
DELI CAFÉ

FONT · NB Grotesk R Black

ABCDEFGHIJKLM
NOPQRSTUVWXYZ
0123456789

COLOR

C0 M20 Y15 K0
C0 M80 Y75 K0
C0 M0 Y0 K0
C0 M0 Y0 K100

GRAPHIC

熱帶
TROPICAL
DELI CAFÉ
TROPICAL
DELI CAFÉ
熱
帶
02-23772208
tropicaldelicafe.com
台北市大安區
和平東路二段134號

TROPICAL
DELI CAFÉ
招待券
憑券兌換
熱帶精選咖啡一杯
熱帶
TROPICAL

TROPICAL
DELI CAFÉ

MENU
義式咖啡 Espresso
濃縮 Espresso (H) 120
美式 Americano (H/I) 120
拿鐵 Latte (H/I) 160
手沖 Pour Over Coffee (H) 180
耶加雪菲 Yirgacheffe
曼特寧 Gold Top Mandheling
曼巴 Gold Top Mandheling & Brazil
台灣茶 Formosa Tea (H) 150
台灣紅茶 Formosa Black Tea
台灣金萱茶 Formosa Jin Xuan Tea
台灣炭培烏龍茶 Formosa Charcoal Roasted Loose Leaf Oolong Tea
台灣南投老茶 Formosa Nantou Aged Tea
蜂蜜鮮奶茶 Milk Tea (H/I) 170
冷泡茶 Cold-Brewed Tea (I) 80
氣泡飲 Sparkling Drinks (I) 120
黑糖薑汁 Brown Sugar and Ginger Sparkling
蜂蜜檸檬 Lemonade with Honey Sparkling
熱帶 Tropical Sparkling
玫瑰蘋果醋 Rose and Cider Vinegar Sparkling
蔓越莓果醋 Cranberry Vinegar Sparkling
可爾必思 Calpis Sparkling
咖啡氣泡飲 Espresso Sparkling
DELI 270
自選組合 Deli Box
4 Choices from Hot / Cold Deli
主廚特選 Chef's Box
(依當日食材為主)
甜點 Dessert
(依現場甜點櫃為主)
OTHERS 20
+鮮奶

TROPICAL
DELI CAFÉ

熱
帶
TROPICAL
DELI CAFÉ
tropicaldelicafe.com

熱
帶
TROPICAL

熱 帶
TROPICAL

熱
帶
TROPICAL
DELI CAFÉ

TROPICAL
DELI CAFÉ

Battersea

Design Agency • Pentagram
Creative Direction • Marina Willer
Design • Hamlet Auyeung, Cleber de Campos, Marta Gaspar, Stuart Gough, Ian Osborne
Project Manager • Kate Blewett
Illustration • Hiromi Suzuki
Copywriting • Naresh Ramchandani, Zuleika Sedgley

Battersea is a much-loved charity that cares for dogs and cats in Britain and beyond. Pentagram worked closely with the charity to develop a brand strategy, tone of voice and visual identity that present Battersea as both a compassionate caregiver and a leading authority in animal welfare. Pentagram uses a family of hand-drawn watercolor illustrations to humanely emphasize Battersea's commitment to care for every dog and cat. Retaining Battersea's signature blue, the watercolors—made up of five dogs and five cats—are used in varying combinations, giving Battersea the flexibility to tell a rich and diverse story across all of its platforms.

LOGO

BATTERSEA
HERE FOR EVERY DOG AND CAT

FONT • Franklin Gothic

ABCDEFGHIJKLM
NOPQRSTUVWXYZ
abcdefghijklm
nopqrstuvwxyz
1234567890

COLOR

C90 M80 Y0 K0
C68 M0 Y13 K0
C32 M26 Y29 K3
C7 M3 Y5 K8

GRAPHIC

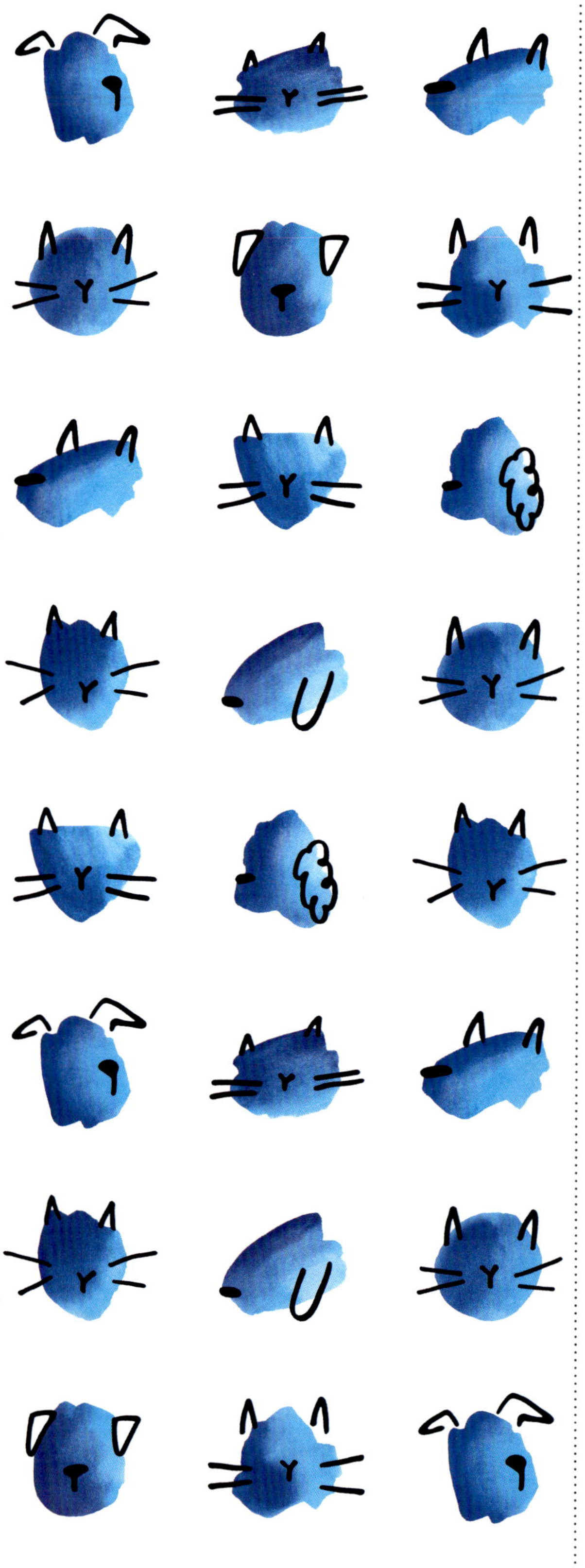

BATTERSEA

MUDDY DOG
A BATTERSEA CHALLENGE
SATURDAY 7 JULY
HENBURY HALL, MANCHESTER
GET MUDDY WITH YOUR DOG FOR OTHER DOGS
MUDDY DOG
A BATTERSEA CHALLENGE
MUDDY DOG
A BATTERSEA CHALLENGE
SATURDAY 18 AUGUST
COEDARHYDYGLYN PARK, CARDIFF
MUDDY DOG CHALLENGE
MUDDY DOG
A BATTERSEA CHALLENGE

Better Breads

Design Agency • **Diferente**
Photography • **Lynn Chen**

Better Breads is a small vegan bakery, where bakers daily prepare different bread varieties that stand out for being vegan, nutritious, organic and fresh, to achieve the goal of feeding customers' bodies and souls through bread. The challenge for Diferente was to create a totally new image that could convey the differential value of the products. The symbol built from the letter B emphasizes the unique quality of its bread. Key elements of the symbol are taken as a reference to develop the entire identity system of the brand, creating a proper language for the bakery that is implemented both in its communications and in the bread packaging system.

LOGO

FONT • Geomanist-Medium

ABCDEFGHIJKLM
NOPQRSTUVWXYZ
abcdefghijklm
nopqrstuvwxyz

COLOR

C80 M45 Y15 K50
C3 M16 Y53 K0
C23 M32 Y0 K0
C22 M0 Y40 K0

GRAPHIC

Better
Breads.
A. 01-37 ONE NORTH RESIDENCES,
SINGAPORE 138643.
T. 0065 9736 8827
E. HI@BETTERBREADS.ORG
W. BETTERBREADS.ORG
I. @BETTERBREADS007
THE SUPER VEGAN BAKERY

BetterBreads.
Nº01
Orange Delight
Orange zest &
Sunflower seeds

We know it's
better if it's
delivered fresh

Spread the Sign

Design Agency • **Kurppa Hosk**

The number of hearing-impaired people in the world is estimated at 70 million but there is no universal sign language—there are hundreds of versions. To facilitate communication, spreadthesign.com is documenting and sharing all of these languages. Kurppa Hosk was asked to create a brand platform and a visual identity for this important initiative. To articulate the overall mission of "Giving everyone the right to a language," Kurppa Hosk created a visual identity that focused on the most essential tool for sign language—the hand—thereby creating a visual expression that challenges common conceptions of handicapped and hearing-impaired tools.

LOGO

SPREAD
THE
SIGN

FONT • Custom Font

SPREAD
THE
SIGN

COLOR

C0 M35 Y90 K0

C0 M0 Y0 K100

C0 M0 Y0 K0

GRAPHIC

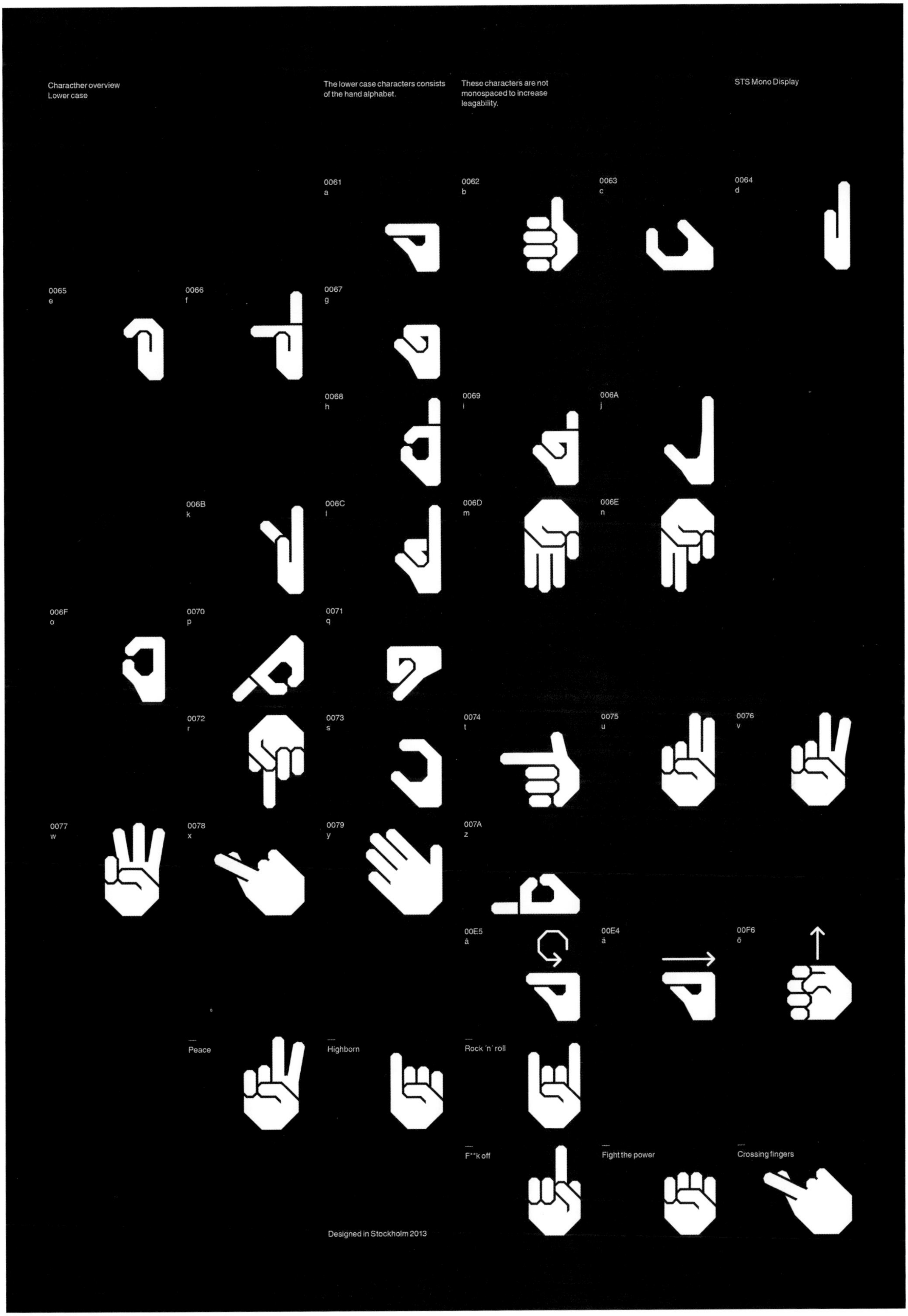

Characther overview
Lower case
The lower case characters consists of the hand alphabet.
These characters are not monospaced to increase leagability.
STS Mono Display
0061 a
0062 b
0063 c
0064 d
0065 e
0066 f
0067 g
0068 h
0069 i
006A j
006B k
006C l
006D m
006E n
006F o
0070 p
0071 q
0072 r
0073 s
0074 t
0075 u
0076 v
0077 w
0078 x
0079 y
007A z
00E5 å
00E4 ä
00F6 ö
Peace
Highborn
Rock 'n' roll
F**k off
Fight the power
Crossing fingers
Designed in Stockholm 2013

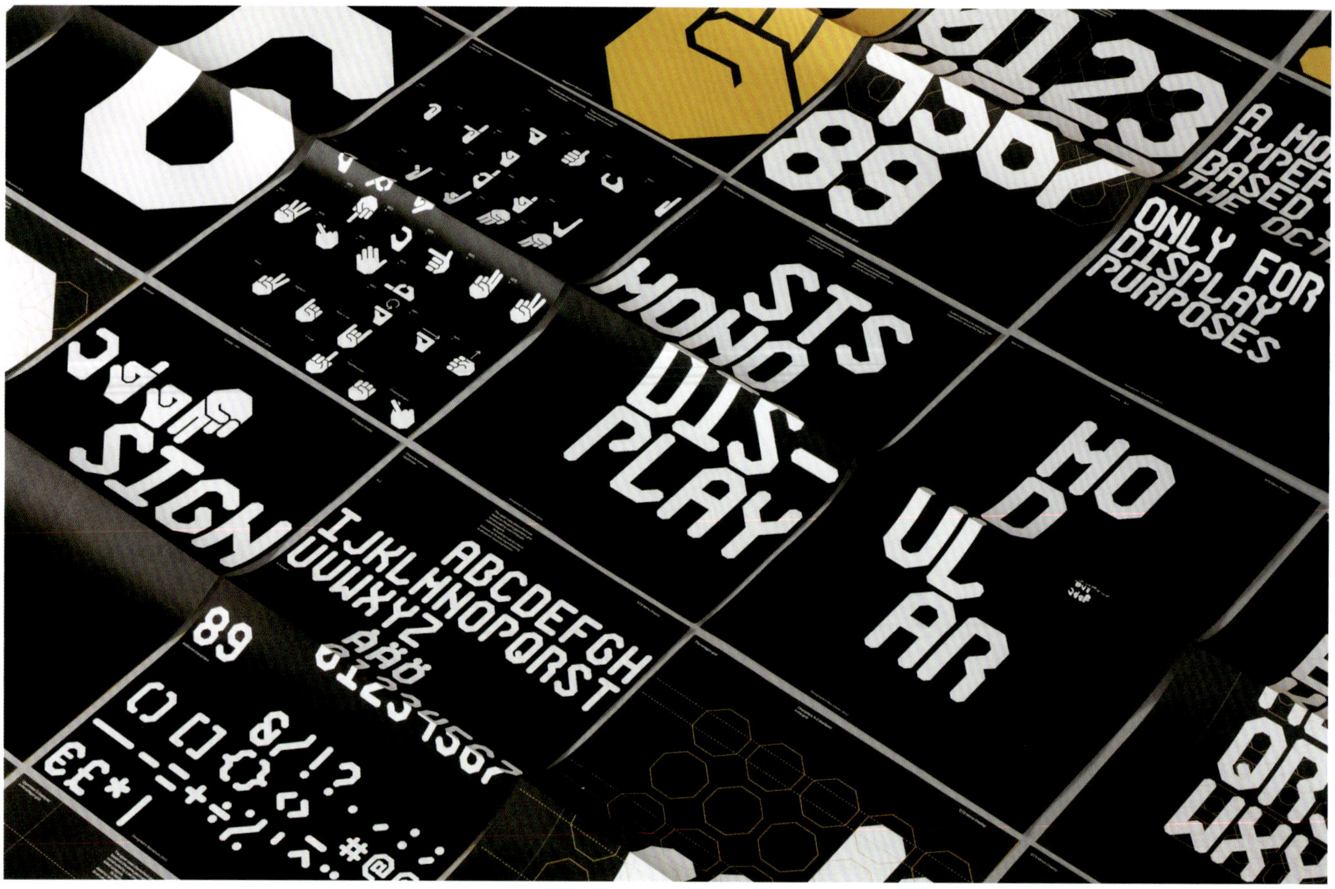
STS
MONO
DIS-
PLAY
MO
D
UL
AR
ONLY FOR
DISPLAY
PURPOSES
SIGN
ABCDEFGH
IJKL MNOPQRST
UVWXYZ
ÅÄÖ
0123
4567
89

spreadthesign.com

HONG KONG
TOKYO
SINGAPORE
TALLIN
NEW DELHI

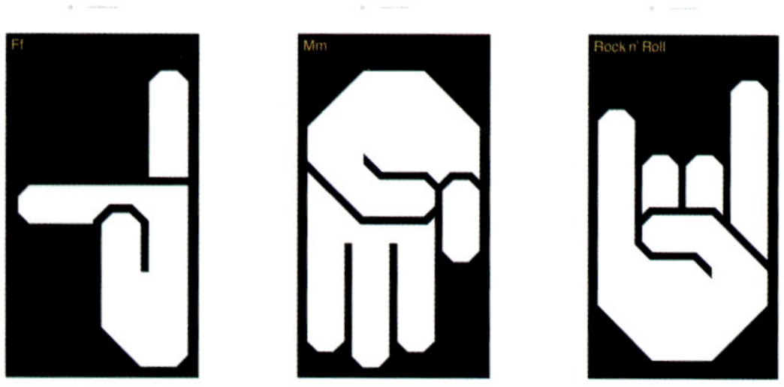
F!
Mm
Rock n' Roll

Home
About
Sign alphabet
Statistics
Spread the sign
Change language
English
SEARCH 167.809 SIGN LANGUAGE VIDEOS IN OUR DATABASE — WELCOME TO SPREAD THE SIGN!
European Sign Language Center
©2013

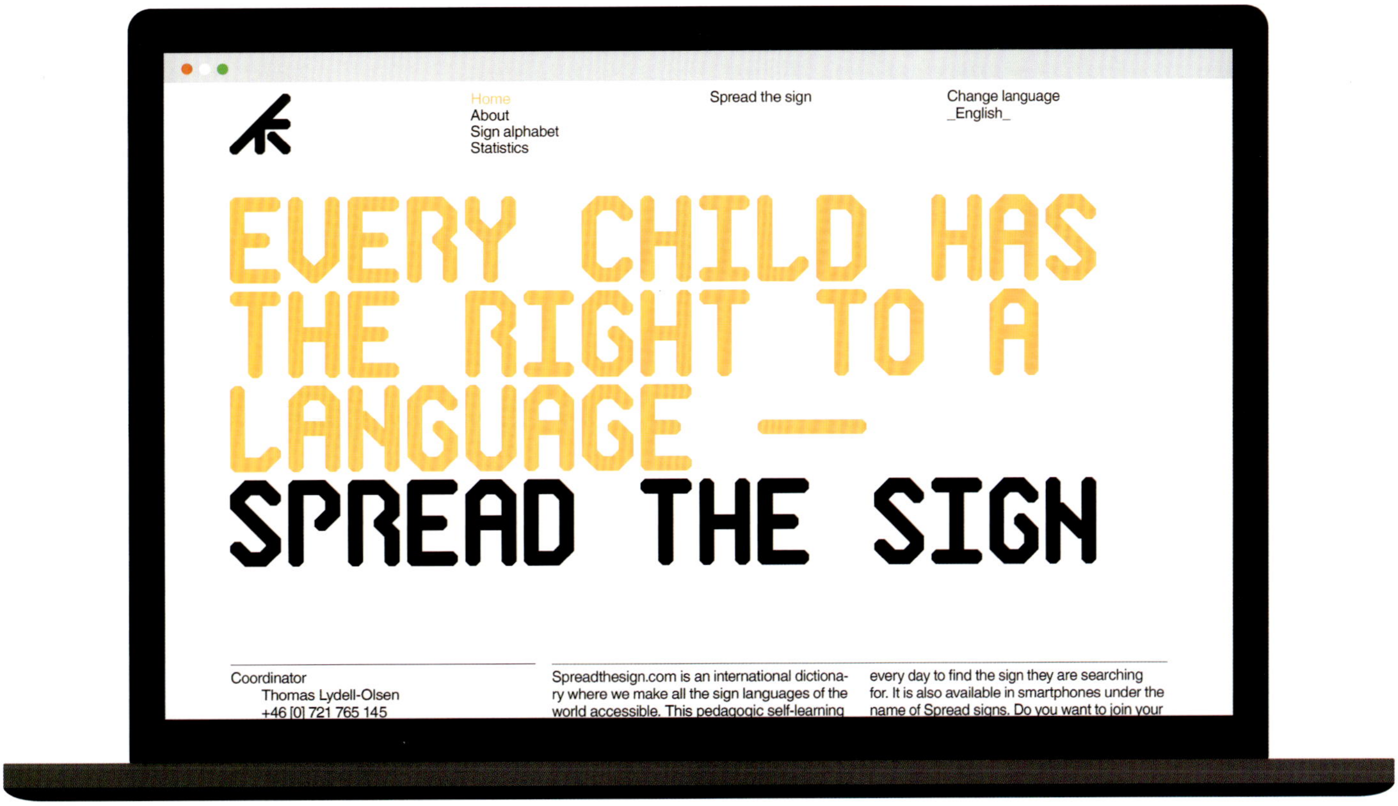
Home
About
Sign alphabet
Statistics
Spread the sign
Change language
English
EVERY CHILD HAS THE RIGHT TO A LANGUAGE —
SPREAD THE SIGN
Coordinator
Thomas Lydell-Olsen
+46 [0] 721 765 145
Spreadthesign.com is an international dictiona-ry where we make all the sign languages of the world accessible. This pedagogic self-learning
every day to find the sign they are searching for. It is also available in smartphones under the name of Spread signs. Do you want to join your

Alternaut Collective

Design • **Petr Kudlacek**

Alternaut Collective is a multidisciplinary independent creative collective focusing mainly on audio-visual and performative work. Petr Kudlacek devised the concept of the brand and created a visual identity based on the collective's film productions.

LOGO

COLLECTIVE

Alternaut

FONT • Wallop

Wallop Light
Wallop Medium
Wallop Bold

COLOR

C10 M25 Y90 K0

C0 M0 Y0 K100

C0 M0 Y0 K0

GRAPHIC

Alternaut
COLLECTIVE
Alternaut
Luxiom
námět - Jiří Horenský
dop - Norman Kudláček
střih - Michal Novotný
produkce - Klára Drsná
námět
casting
do 9. 4.
výběr lokací
do 10. 4.
postprodukce
do 14. 4.
střih
10. 4. - 13. 4.
deadline
16. 4.
schedule
cast

Alternaut
Změnit kurz a vybočit ze své oběžné dráhy není jednoduché. Je k tomu potřeba odstranit to co nám stojí v cestě. Proletět atmosférou, kde toho sice většina shoří, ale to co přežije za to rozhodně stojí.
latest work
say hello
+420 723 727 251
Alternaut 2017, Janovského 12, Praha 7, 170 00
rnaut
Alternaut
Alternaut

Tyche

Design Agency • **Bruch—Idee&Form**
Art Direction • **Bruch—Idee&Form**
Photography • **Daniel Gebhart de Koekkoek**

The "yips," a term popularized by the former golf champion Tommy Armour, is the loss of fine motor skills in athletes. The "yips" affects nearly one-half of all mature golfers. Thus the start-up Tyche developed a product that helps golfers to control their movements and to get their game back again. A clear and highly intelligible corporate identity was essential to differentiate the brand from the market's competitors. Large amounts of white space with green accents and plain typography in combination with very bold and eye-catching visuals communicate the therapeutic product in a serious and also striking way.

LOGO

TYCHE

FONT · Hermes

ABCDEFGHIJKLM
NOPQRSTUVWXYZ
abcdefghijklm
nopqrstuvwxyz
1234567890

COLOR

C0 M0 Y0 K0

C80 M0 Y75 K0

GRAPHIC

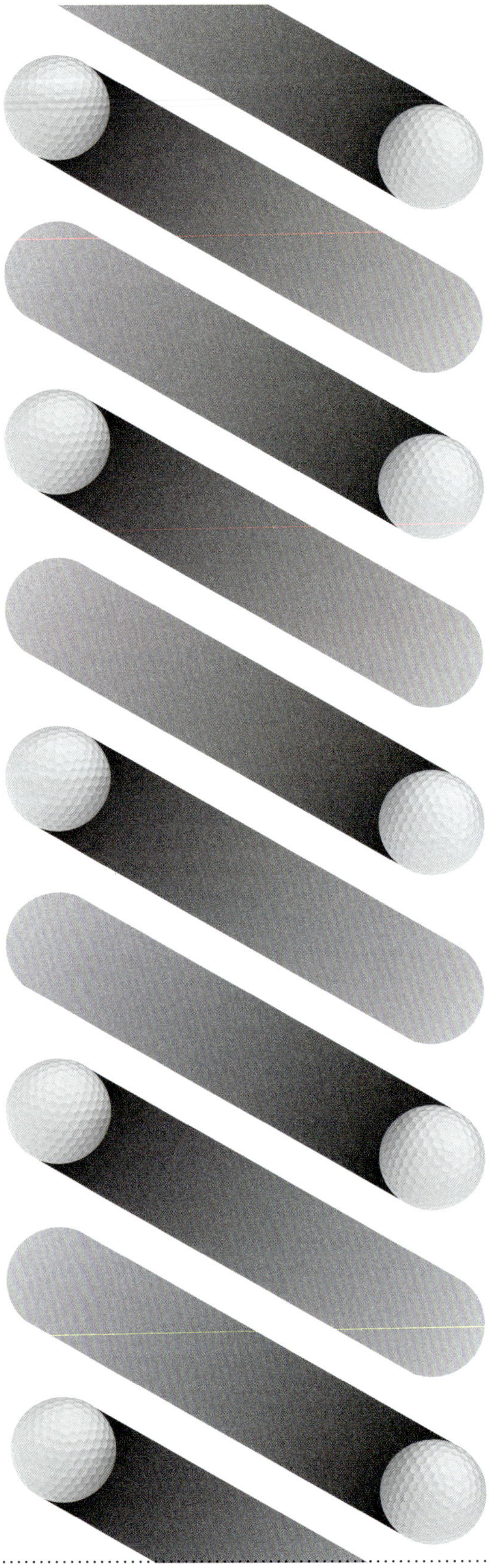

TYCHE
TYCHE Technologies GmbH
Esterhazygasse 15/15
1060 Wien, Österreich
+41 78 610 02 77
info@tychegolf.com
www.tychegolf.com

TYCHE
Get your game back.

7 Steps for getting back your game.
Operating Manual
TYCHE

Biomatica

Design • **Masha Knop**

Biomatica is a shop in Saint Petersburg that focuses on unique, organic products from all over the world. Smooth lines, round shapes, pastel colors and natural fabrics are the brand's base. The main purpose for designers was to create a fresh look and feel with a minimal usage of graphic elements.

GRAPHIC

LOGO

BIOMATICA

FONT · CRC

ABCDEFGHIJKLM
NOPQRSTUVWXYZ
abcdefghijklm
nopqrstuvwxyz
1234567890

COLOR

C40 M15 Y55 K0
C0 M20 Y65 K0
C0 M30 Y45 K0
C60 M70 Y45 K30

ЕСЛИ ХОЧЕТСЯ ...
БАЗИЛИК
ЕСЛИ ХОЧЕТСЯ ...

BIO
MATICA
ОРГАНИЧЕСКИЕ
ПРОДУКТЫ
BIO
MATICA
ОРГАНИЧЕСКИЕ
ПРОДУКТЫ

BIOMATICA
ОРГАНИЧЕСКИЕ ПРОДУКТЫ

BIOMATICA
ОРГАНИЧЕСКИЕ ПРОДУКТЫ
Скидка 3%
если приходите
со своей экосумкой
Дегустация
новых продуктов
каждую неделю
Скидки
на лучшие товары
месяца

Real Jardín Botánico de Madrid

Design Agency • **The Woork Co.**
Art Direction • **The Woork Co.**
Client • **Real Jardín Botánico de Madrid**

With the objective of attracting younger audiences and broadcasting a living museum image, The Woork Co. renewed the whole institutional identity of Real Jardín Botánico de Madrid. Designers worked with monospaced typographies, reminiscent of printed museum entries. They also chose a wide color palette, escaping from the traditional shades derived from the color studies of Thaddeus Haenke's botany. For the logo, they worked on the simplest way to represent three leaves, a crown, and a museum entrance door. Deconstructing the symbol, The Woork Co. generated a new iconography and brand illustration style.

LOGO

Real
Jardín
Botánico

FONT · DecimaMonoX

ABCDEFGHIJKLM
NOPQRSTUVWXYZ
abcdefghijklm
nopqrstuvwxyz
1234567890

COLOR

C63 M0 Y38 K0
C50 M0 Y100 K0
C0 M40 Y88 K0

GRAPHIC

29 Y 30
DE ABRIL
Real
Jardín
Botánico
Especialización
en poda de
especies
arbustivas y
rosales
CSIC

Real
Jardín
Botánico

Real
Jardín
Botánico
09 ABRIL AL
07 MAYO 2017
Raíces del
Expresionismo
Experimental
RAMÓN JUAN
CSIC

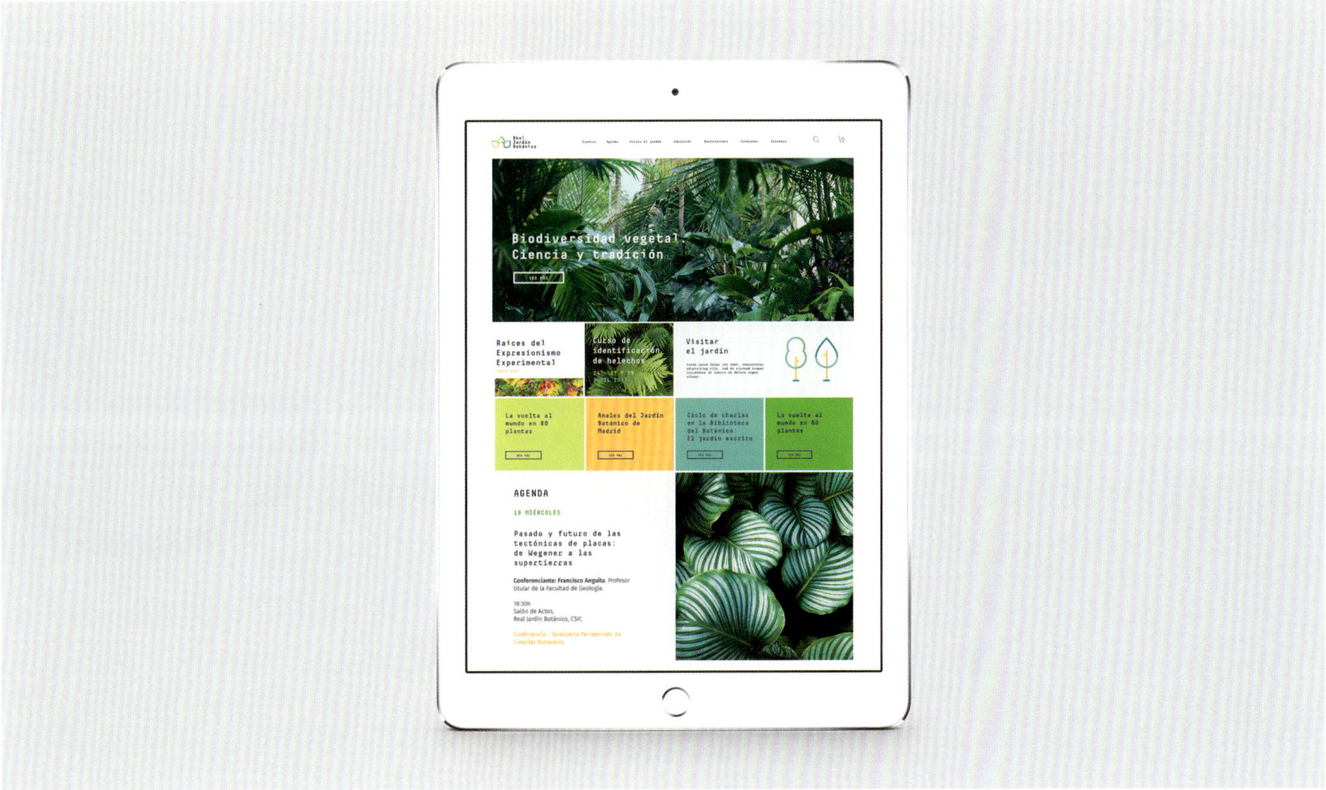
Biodiversidad vegetal.
Ciencia y tradición
Raíces del
Expresionismo
Experimental
Curso de
identificación
de helechos
Visitar
el jardín
La vuelta al
mundo en 80
plantas
Anales del Jardín
Botánico de
Madrid
Ciclo de charlas
en la Biblioteca
del Botánico:
El jardín escrito
La vuelta al
mundo en 80
plantas
AGENDA
19 MIÉRCOLES
Pasado y futuro de las
tectónicas de placas:
de Wegener a las
supertierras
Conferenciante: Francisco Anguita. Profesor
titular de la Facultad de Geología.
18:30h
Salón de Actos,
Real Jardín Botánico, CSIC

Sushiroll

Design Agency • **DekoRatio Branding & Design Studio**
Design • **Zsofia Nagy**

Sushiroll introduces a whole new concept to the ever-changing gastronomy scene in Budapest: sushi as street food. Their uncut sushi rolls are ready to take away in seconds and they can easily be eaten on the go. DekoRatio Branding & Design Studio's aim was to create a friendly and approachable design that shows another exciting way of eating sushi that might be able to convert some avowed sushi haters. The parentheses in the logo not only suggest the endless possibilities—you can put almost anything in their rolls—but also create the appearance of an actual sushi roll. Zsofia also used a hint of Japanese culture in the typography.

LOGO

(sushiroll)

FONT · Brandon bld

ABCDEFGHIJKLM
NOPQRSTUVWXYZ
abcdefghijklm
nopqrstuvwxyz
1234567890

COLOR

C0 M30 Y35 K0   C100 M0 Y0 K90

GRAPHIC

KEEP ROLLIN'

KEEP ROLLIN'
(SUSHIroll)
KEEP ROLLIN'
KEEP ROLLIN'

ALL YOU
NEED IS LOVE.
SUSHIROLLS.
KEEP ROLLIN'

Phu Quoc Sea Gift

Design Agency • **GM Creative Studio**
Design • **Kien Tran, Tin Lai, Hieu Le, Linh Tran, Buun Ngo**
Client • **PQSG**
Photography • **Nam Nguyen**

Phu Quoc Sea Gift was born as a unique combination of high-quality seafood and the finest natural ingredients from Phu Quoc Island, such as pepper and fish sauce. Every day, their skillful chefs follow strict recipes that use traditional methods combined with Japanese technology to create delicious and nutritious seafood snacks.

LOGO

FONT • Loew-Heavy

ABCDEFGHIJKLM
NOPQRSTUVWXYZ
abcdefghijklm
nopqrstuvwxyz
1234567890

COLOR

C100 M100 Y0 K25
C0 M80 Y95 K0
C0 M0 Y0 K0

GRAPHIC

PHU QUOC
SEA GIFT

PHU QUOC
SEA GIFT
CÁ THIỀU NƯỚNG
GRILLED FISH
TÔM
SHRIMP
BÁNH
SNACK MỰC
SQUID
SNACK
INGREDIENTS / THÀNH PHẦN
MỰC, BỘT MÌ, GIA VỊ
SQUID, FLOUR, SEASONING
BUTTER FLAVOR
VỊ BƠ
BÁNH
SNACK CÁ
FISH
SNACK
TIÊU SỌ
PHÚ QUỐC
WHOLE WHITE PEPPER
TIÊU ĐEN
PHÚ QUỐC

MỰC NƯỚNG
TẨM GIA VỊ
ROLLED ROASTED SQUID
ORIGINAL
FLAVOR
CÁ THIỀU NƯỚNG
CÁT SỢI
GRILLED FISH SNACK
INGREDIENTS / THANH PHAN

BÁNH
HẢI SẢN
NƯỚNG
PHÚ QUỐC
かいせんせんべい
PHU QUOC CRISPY
SEAFOOD CRACKER
PHU QUOC
SEA GIFT
ORIGINAL
FLAVOR
PHU QUOC
SEA GIFT

Salami & Co.

Art Direction • **Oscar Bastidas**
Design • **Oscar Bastidas**
Illustration • **Oscar Bastidas**
Photography • **Oscar Bastidas, Salami & Co., Nathan Dumlao, Kate Remmer**

Salami & Co. is a pet-friendly coffee shop located in Yorkshire, UK. Oscar had the opportunity to develop the logo, menu, and packaging. "Salami" is the name of the shop pet, a friendly dachshund who greets visitors to this special coffee house.

LOGO

SALAMI & CO.
COFFEE HOUSE

FONT • Nevis

ABCDEFGHIJKLM
NOPQRSTUVWXYZ
abcdefghijklmnopqrst
uvwxyz 1234567890

COLOR

C74 M67 Y67 K90 CO MO YO KO

GRAPHIC

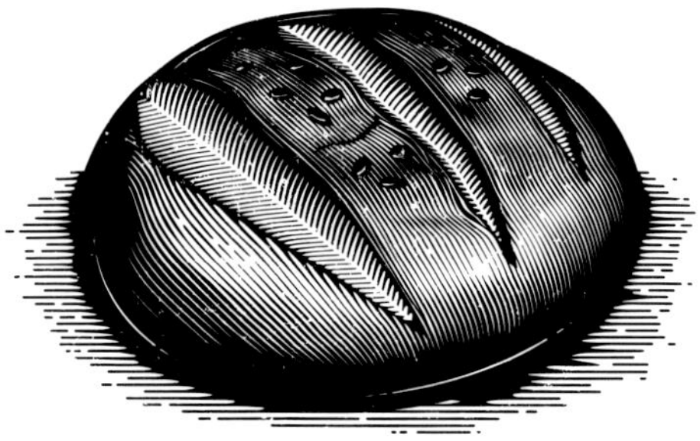

SALAMI&CO.
COFFEE HOUSE

SALAMI&CO.
COFFEE HOUSE

SALAMI&CO.
COFFEE HOUSE

SALAMI&CO
COFFEE HOUSE

Clear Optics

Design • Anthony Lam
Client • Clear Optics Company Limited

Anthony Lam designed a simple and remarkable logo for an optical shop—the glasses' frames form the shop's initials. The visual identity, which was applied across multiple marketing materials, uses primary colors, the signature "Happy Face" graphics, and eye-catching photo montages to convey a clear vision through stylish and personal eyewear.

LOGO

Clear Optics 目清光學

FONT • Now

ABCDEFGHIJKLM
NOPQRSTUVWXYZ
abcdefghijklm
nopqrstuvwxyz
1234567890

COLOR

C95 M65 Y0 K0
C0 M95 Y100 K0
C0 M0 Y0 K0
C0 M0 Y100 K0

GRAPHIC

Clear Optics
目清光學
Eyewear
Eye Check-up
Glaucoma Screening Examination
Macular Disease Screening Examniation
Adult Eye Examination
Children Eye Examination
Refraction
Clear Optics Company Limited
Shop No. 171, Level 1, Park Central,
No. 9 Tong Tak Street,
Tsueng Kwan O
電話 2660 7680 / 2660 7828
傳真 2663 2883

Samán Arepas

Design Agency • **WePropagate**
Art Direction • **Oscar Bastidas**
Design • **Oscar Bastidas**
Photography • **Oscar Bastidas, Samán Arepas, Gaelle Marcel**

In 2017 the Venezuelan restaurant Samán Arepas decided to expand and completely change its commercial identity. Oscar Bastidas was in charge of the new graphics, creative concept, logo re-design, stationery, promotional materials, uniforms, facade and also the brand's "personality." He used the samán, a Venezuelan tree, as the main element behind the restaurant's graphic story—a story that merges Venezuelan insights with a touch of fantasy.

LOGO

FONT • Custom Font

ABCDEFGHIJKLM
NOPQRSTUVWXYZ
1234567890

COLOR

C30 M0 Y100 K0

C0 M85 Y55 K0

C0 M0 Y0 K0

GRAPHIC

J.BLANCO
3052032259
JBLANCO@SAMANAREPAS.COM
SAMANAREPAS
SAMĀN
AREPAS

AREPAS

SAMĀN
AREPAS
SAMANAREPAS

SAMĀN
AREPAS

THE EFFECTS OF
Arepa
PELUA

THE STORY OF THE
IADA

THE BEST
AREPAS
IN Town

venezuelan
FOOD
IS TRENDY
SAMĀN
AREPAS

SAMĀN
AREPAS
SAMANAREPAS.COM
SAMANAREPAS

Voluntourism Programme

Design Agency • **Untitled Macao**
Art Direction • **Si Ngalan**
Creative Direction • **Au Chon Hin**
Design • **Lao Chon Hong**

Through International Workcamp, volunteers undertake working journeys, gaining work experience and forming connections as they work to improve lives along the way. Through a series of illustrations that describe the process of volunteering, the design identity reveals the core of the concept.

LOGO

COMMUNICATE WITH THE WORLD!

FONT • Touche

ABCDEFGHIJKLM
NOPQRSTUVWXYZ
abcdefghijklm
nopqrstuvwxyz
1234567890

COLOR

C90 M0 Y75 K75

C20 M0 Y15 K0

C0 M0 Y0 K0

GRAPHIC

APPLICATION PROCEDURE
報名流程
COMMUNICATE WITH THE WORLD!
MNCYA INTERNATIONAL WORKCAMP
VOLUNTOURISM
志遊人計劃
PROGRAMME
VOLUNTOURISM PROGRAMME
PARTICIPANTS' SHARING
分享

COMMUNICATE WITH THE WORLD!

Churrasqueria

Design Agency • **Estudio Altillo**
Art Direction • **Estudio Altillo**

Meat, fire, and vermouth are traditions that Argentinians pass from one generation to another. All are equally valued. Churrasqueria proposes to value Argentinian food and to treat every raw material with respect, bringing a certain nobility to the table. The space is relaxed, with a special emphasis on "Vermouth Time."

LOGO

CHURRASQUERIA

FONT · GearedSlab

A B C D E F G H I J K L M
N O P Q R S T U V W X Y Z
a b c d e f g h i j k l m
n o p q r s t u v w x y z
1234567890

COLOR

C0 M0 Y0 K0

C99 M86 Y36 K27

GRAPHIC

CHURRASQUERIA

CINZANO
#HOYVERMUT

CHURRASQUERIA
CARNE Y VERMUT PARA TODA LA GENTE
COMIDA HONESTA
MARZO
3
VIERNES
BEBIDAS NOBLES
CATAMARCA ESQ. DORREGO - ROSARIO - ARGENTINA
MARZO 2017
REGISTRO ANUAL DE LLUVIAS

ROSARIO: ARG
COMIDAS DE CHURRASQUERIA
CARNES Y BEBIDAS NOBLES
BEBER RESPONSABLEMENTE
FRIOS
CARNES
CALIENTES
VEGETALES ASADOS
CONSERVAS
ENSALADAS
CHURRASQUERIA

BIENVENIDOS
CHURRASQUERIA

CARNE Y VERMUT
TODA LA

CHURRASQUERIA

URRAS
IERIA
MUT
GENTE

Balthazar Eyewear

Art Direction • Simon Piu
Design • Simon Piu
Photography • Simon Piu

Balthazar is an optician based in Aix-en-Provence, France, who sells his own models of glasses, both optical and sunglasses. The colors of the brand identity convey the made-in-France idea and the roundness of the logotype and typefaces bring friendliness and affordability to the brand. Simon created illustrations, representing a variety of people, so everyone can identify with the brand. These identities and illustrations also appear throughout the store.

LOGO

Balthazar
AIX-EN-PROVENCE

FONT · CooperBlackStd

A B C D E F G H I J K L M N
O P Q R S T U V W X Y Z
a b c d e f g h i j k l m n
o p q r s t u v w x y z
1 2 3 4 5 6 7 8 9 0 ! ? @ #
° & / ( ) = + * % , . : ;

COLOR

C100 M90 Y22 K4 C2 M95 Y86 K0

GRAPHIC

Balthazar
Aix-en-Provence

Balthazar
AIX-EN-PROVENCE
1 rue Gaston de Saporta
13100 Aix-en-Provence
04 42 23 03 92
www.lunettes-balthazar.fr
MES MODÈLES ESSAYÉS

Balthazar
AIX-EN-PROVENCE
OPTICIEN
OPTIQUES
SOLAIRES
LUNETTES
MADE IN
FRANCE
10H-19H
Du mardi au samedi

Solaires
Balthazar
Vous souhaite la bienvenue !
Rejoignez-nous sur les réseaux :

Spongie

Design Agency • **Luminous Design Group**
Client • **Bitos Flex**

The logo design of "Spongie" was based on the friendly and playful feeling people have with a sponge. This sense was expanded by the creation of a series of illustrations for each product, stressing its particular use.

LOGO

FONT • Averta-Black

ABCDEFGHIJKLM
NOPQRSTUVWXYZ
abcdefghijklm
nopqrstuvwxyz
1234567890

COLOR

C60 M0 Y10 K0
C60 M0 Y100 K0
C80 M100 Y0 K0
C0 M0 Y0 K100

GRAPHIC

BATH GLOVE
Massage
Soft
SPONGIE
Skin Refreshner
Scrub and wash your body with massage effects.
NO 212
BODY SPONGE
Exfoliating
Gentle cleansing, designed for smooth & radiant skin.
NO 214
SPONGIE
Skin Refreshner
BODY SPONGE
Soft
For sensitive skins, creates a relaxing and gentle effect on the skin.
NO 213
SPONGIE
Skin Refreshner
KIDS
BODY SPONGE
FOR OUR LITTLE HEROES
SOFT
NO 226
SPONGIE
Skin Refreshner
BODY SPONGE
Massage
Soft
Scrub and wash your body with massage effects.
NO 217
SPONGIE
Skin Refreshner
BODY SPONGE
Hydro
Soft
Fine pore cell structure, super water-absorption.
NO 220
SPONGIE
Skin Refreshner

6th & 7th Record & CD Fairs in Seoul

Design Agency • **Studio fnt**
Art Direction • **Jaemin Lee**
Design • **Jaemin Lee**

The Record & CD Fair, in Seoul, was the first domestic sale event to feature record labels, musicians and music fans. Studio fnt's job was to art-direct the visual language and graphics for the whole event, including teaser and main posters, banners, postcards, fliers, web banners, leaflets, signage, etc. The event brings many different vendors each year and it was important that the main graphics be strong enough to represent all the individual labels. Studio fnt simply used the solid black of vinyl records as a graphic motif, which also helped the organizers to minimize the cost of production by using just one color for printing.

LOGO

서울 레코드 페어 ™

FONT · Trade Gothic

A B C D E F G H I J K L M
N O P Q R S T U V W X Y Z
a b c d e f g h i j k l m
n o p q r s t u v w x y z
1234567890

COLOR

● C0 M0 Y0 K100 ○ C0 M0 Y0 K0

GRAPHIC

2017 서울레코드페어 "사이드 B"
2017 RECORD & CD FAIR IN SEOUL "SIDE B"
서울혁신파크 SEOUL INNOVATION PARK
11. 11. SATURDAY
www.recordfair.kr
facebook.com/recordfair
instagram: @seoul_recordfair

EN-
TRAN
CE
서울
레코드
페어
2층 행사장으로
올라가세요

SMOKING
AREA

RECORD
& CD
FAIR IN
SEOUL
2017. 6.
17 – 18

Visual Identity of Kaunas 1st School of Music

Design • Aurėja Jucevičiūtė
Client • Vilnius Academy of Arts Faculty of Kaunas

The logo of Kaunas 1st School of Music has an abstract style and was created by combining different geometrical shapes. The strict and sharp shapes were chosen to develop a different approach to music visualization. The logo is composed of the musical stave and other dynamic forms, which symbolizes education and freedom of music and creativity. The logic and concept of the logo structure also reveal the whole learning process: In order to improvise students first have to learn certain rules. Emphasis was placed on the rectangle shape in the center of the logo, which highlights the uniqueness of the school. The gold color is also an allusion to some musical instruments and their luster.

LOGO

KAUNO
PIRMOJI
MUZIKOS
MOKYKLA

FONT BenchNine

ABCDEFGHIJKLM
NOPQRSTUVWXYZ
abcdefghijklm
nopqrstuvwxyz
1234567890

COLOR

C0 M0 Y0 K100
C17 M18 Y54 K0
C0 M0 Y0 K0

GRAPHIC

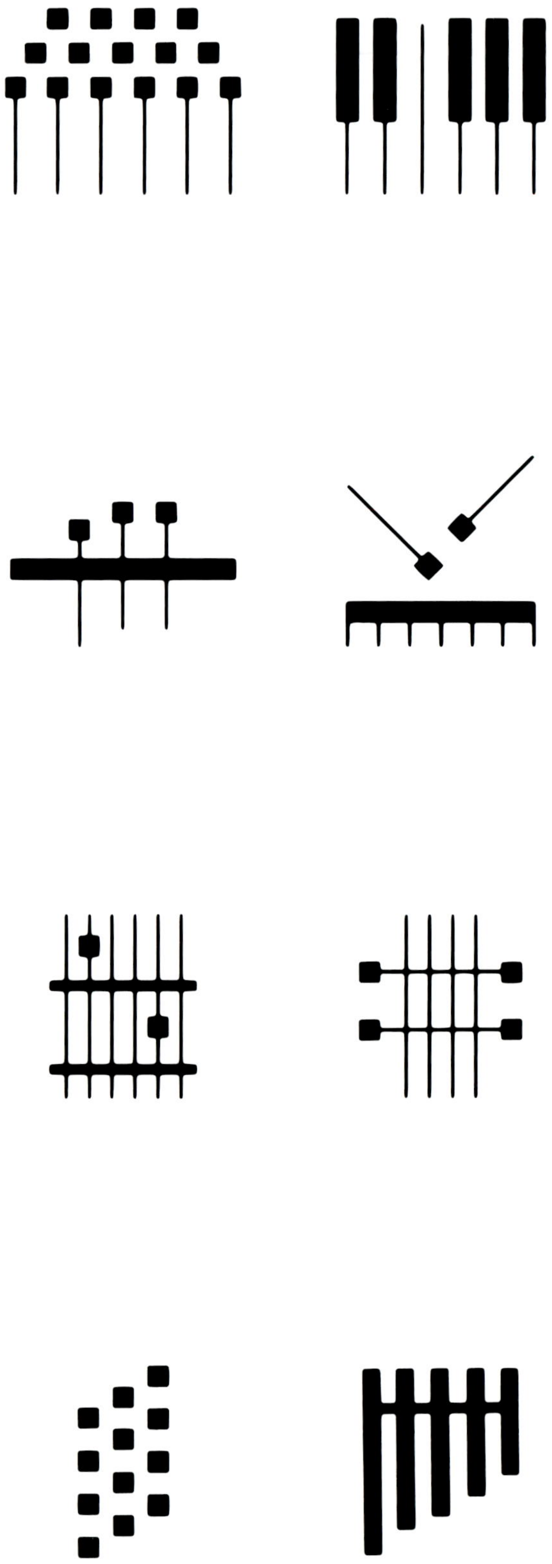

DIPLOMAS

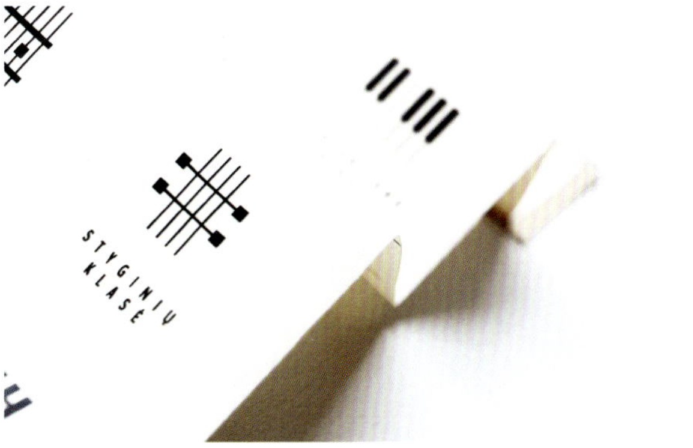
STYGINIŲ KLASĖ

KAUNO
PIRMOJI
MUZIKOS
MOKYKLA

KAUNO
PIRMOJI
MUZIKOS
MOKYKLA

Miavana: Island Sanctuary

Design Agency • **Xfacta**
Client • **Time+Tide**

Miavana is an exclusive, ultra-luxury eco-destination located on Nosy Ankao, an island sanctuary off the Madagascan mainland. Xfacta's task was to develop every aspect of the brand. In Malagasy, *miavana* means "to reconcile." Informed by the rhythm and flow of Mother Nature, Xfacta created the Miavana logotype. The considered proportions and curves of the letterforms are inspired by the Indian Ocean's rippling waves as they meet the pristine beaches. Xfacta honored nature's artistry and sought to mimic it in their design. The colors of rich copper and turquoise are drawn from the island's abundant coral reefs, flawless beaches, and shimmering ocean. The island's French heritage was reflected in bold Breton stripes, while local flora and fauna were depicted in the style of traditional Madagascan woodcuts.

LOGO

MIAVANA

ISLAND SANCTUARY
NOSY ANKAO MADAGASCAR

FONT • MuseoSans-900

ABCDEFGHIJKLM
NOPQRSTUVWXYZ
abcdefghijklm
nopqrstuvwxyz
1234567890

COLOR

C60 M5 Y30 K0

C39 M0 Y35 K0

GRAPHIC

MIAVANA

FOOD FOR THOUGHT
GOOD MORNING
FACT OF THE DAY
Blueberry Pancakes
MIAVANA

PIZZA

MIAVANA
NOSY ANKAO MADAGASCAR
MIAVANA
NOSY ANKAO MADAGASCAR

MIAVANA

MIAVANA

Reggie's Barber Shop

Design • **Tina Homewood**

The concept for Reggie's Barber Shop was to develop a warm and welcoming brand that would be accessible to all age groups. Using the traditional barbershop colors of red, white and blue while incorporating the iconic striped barbershop pole, Tina Homewood was able to establish an illustrative and playful style. The illustrations create catchy visuals that could be used and adapted across the brand, creating a strong and recognizable identity. Extending the brand further she used a display typeface with more traditional ones to emphasize the brand's message of a fun but quality service.

LOGO

Reggie's
BARBER SHOP
–1984–

FONT • BodoniStd

ABCDEFGHIJKLM
NOPQRSTUVWXYZ
abcdefghijklm
nopqrstuvwxyz
1234567890

COLOR

C100 M76 Y23 K8
C1 M89 Y100 K0
C0 M68 Y49 K0
C78 M32 Y0 K0

GRAPHIC

Reggie's
BARBER SHOP

SENIOR CITIZENS
30% OFF OF ALL SERVICES
MONDAY-WEDNESDAY
(OVER 65)
KIDS CUT
UNDER 5s £5.00
JUNIOR £10.00
10%
OFF OF ALL SERVICES
FOR LOCAL BUSINESSES
ALL DAY MON-WED
15%
OFF OF ALL
SHAVING PRODUCTS
ON FRIDAYS WITH ANY
BEARD TREATMENT
20%
OFF FOR ALL
QUALIFYING STUDENTS
ON ALL SERVICES
MONDAYS ONLY
LUX
£40.00
A haircut followed by a
hot-towel shave... One of
life's little luxuries.
£6.00
ISH £2

Reggie's
SHAMPOO
FOR NORMAL TO DRY HAIR
Reggie's
HAIR WAX
FOR ALL HAIR TYPES
Reggie's
HAIR SPRAY
FOR ALL HAIR TYPES
Reggie's
SHAVING FOAM
FOR SENSITIVE SKIN

Maison Gourmande

Design • **Charlotte Got**

Maison Gourmande is a French pastry shop in Taipei, run by a couple. They offer fresh traditional pastries, baked daily, to their customers. Charlotte Got was asked to redesign their global visual identity in a way that would preserve the bakery's aesthetic and create a brand harmony through the different supports. The client wanted an original, simple, and clean look. The solution came through illustrations. By illustrating the main products and symbols related to the brand, Charlotte Got created a unique identity, easily recognizable and adaptable.

LOGO

CANNELÉ
可麗露

FONT • Montserrat

ABCDEFGHIJKLM
NOPQRSTUVWXYZ
abcdefghijklmno
pqrstuvwxyz
0123456789

COLOR

C0 M86 Y69 K0

C84 M65 Y15 K2

C27 M35 Y62 K0

GRAPHIC

MAISON GOURMANDE
PÂTISSERIE

MAISON GOURMANDE
TAKEAWAY

MAISON
GOURMANDE
CANNELÉ

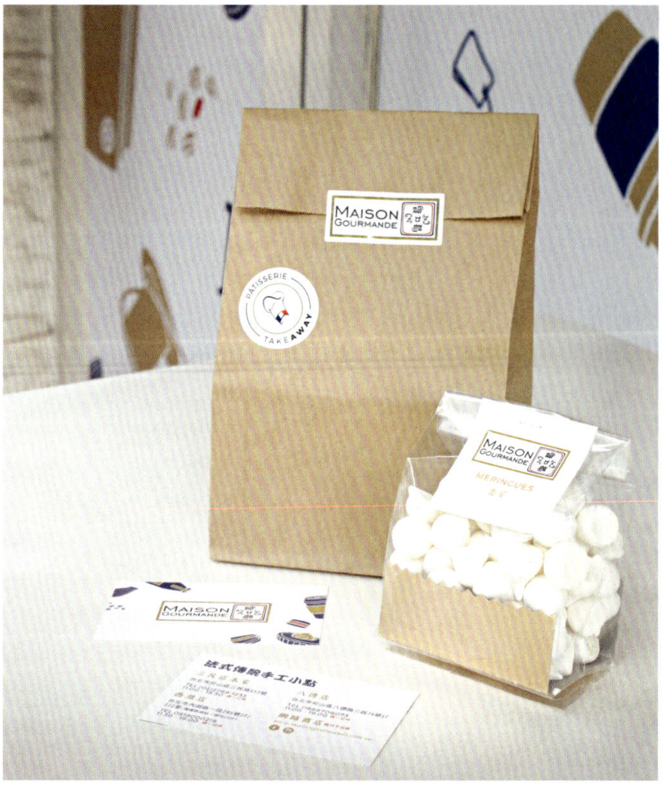
MAISON
GOURMANDE
PATISSERIE
TAKEAWAY
MERINGUES

MAISON
GOURMANDE
添加物及化學色素之馬卡龍，請
儘早食用完畢！請冷藏保存，口感最
佳賞味期為三日，可宅配

只要800元
禮盒帶著走
6 x
2 x
1 x

Robo&Bobo

Design Agency • **Quattrolinee**

Robo&Bobo promotes literacy in the fields of design, electronics, and programming by implementing a series of workshops for teen and preteen patients of the Pediatric Onco-hematology department and Transplant Center of Regina Margherita Hospital, in Turin. The communication strategy developed by Quattrolinee introduces the workshops in a playful way—each lab is represented by a colorful robot that encourages kids to play with technologies.

LOGO

Robo
&Bobo

FONT · Space Mono

ABCDEFGHIJKLM
NOPQRSTUVWXYZ
abcdefghijklm
nopqrstuvwxyz
1234567890

COLOR

C0 M65 Y79 K0
C63 M9 Y81 K0
C60 M49 Y46 K37
C5 M29 Y93 K0

GRAPHIC

Robo
&Bobo
Codix
easy logic coding
www.designaround.org/
www.roboandbobo.designaround.org

ELECTRIC PAINT
Robo
&Bobo
Preent
3-D fun printing
Il laboratorio introduce alla modellazione e alla stampa 3D. Con l'aiuto degli operatori puoi imparare a costruire un modello e a realizzarlo tramite una stampante 3D, ottenendo degli oggetti da conservare.
Robo
&Bobo
Cir-cut
Interactive origami
L'attività affronta il tema dell'elettricità e dei circuiti in modo pratico e ludico: utilizzando nastro adesivo di rame, LED e inchiostro conduttivo, puoi imparare che cosa sono la corrente elettrica, la polarità e i diodi luminosi.
Per saperne di più, visita:
www.roboandbobo.designaround.org
un progetto di
con il sostegno di
Robo
&Bobo
Preent
3-D fun printing
Il laboratorio introduce alla modellazione e alla stampa 3D. Con l'aiuto degli operatori puoi imparare a costruire un modello e a realizzarlo tramite una stampante 3D, ottenendo degli oggetti da conservare.

Robo
&Bobo
Robo
&Bobo
Robo
&Bobo
Introduzio
Un laboratorio di
i partecipanti impara
cosa sono
capacitivo e come
con dei joystick
Per saperne di più
L'attività
in modo
di rame,
imparano
polarità
Eye-oh
Virtual eyes
Manuale del
laboratorio
Il laboratorio è dedicato al disegno vettoriale e alla
realtà virtuale. I partecipanti si esercitano su tablet
a comporre dei disegni
e a costruire dei visori di cartone
apposite app su smartphone.
Per saperne di più, visita:

Joybit
Robo
&Bobo
Manuale del
laboratorio
Cir-cut
Eye-oh
Preent
Robo
&Bobo
Preent
3-D fun printing
ELECTRIC PAINT

ELECTRIC PAINT
Robo &Bobo
Cir-cut
interactive origami
Manuale del laboratorio

Robo &Bobo
un progetto di Dear, Design around

Little Tokyo Identity

Design Agency • **KittoKatsu**

The city of Düsseldorf has one of the biggest Japanese communities in Europe. Little Tokyo is the vibrant center of the city's Japanese cultural life. The goal of this project was to create an identity that would give the district a strong and independent voice. By mixing traditional elements of Japanese culture, such as the *maneki-neko*, with typical Rhineland icons like *Altbier*, the identity reflects the unique cultural fusion characteristic of the district. With a palette of bold colors and strong typographic elements, it becomes playful yet respectful heritage and culture.

LOGO

FONT • Terrazzo

ABCDEFGHIJKLM
NOPQRSTUVWXYZ
abcdefghijklm
nopqrstuvwxyz
1234567890

COLOR

C1 M76 Y61 K0

C100 M86 Y18 K4

C7 M2 Y74 K0

GRAPHIC

Little Tokyo
リトル東京
Düsseldorf・デュッセルドルフ
www.tokyodorf.com

エビ
アルト

Little Tokyo
リトル東京
Karneval
カーニバル
Karneval
カーニバル
Karneval
カーニバル
Karneval
www.tokyodorf.com

Little Tokyo
リトル東京
www.tokyodorf.com

STRÖER
Liesegangstraße
16–24
リトル東京
招き猫
Karneval
カーニバル
Karneval
カーニバル
Karneval
カーニバル
Karneval

Little Tokyo
リトル東京
Sake
酒
www.tokyodorf.com
Little Tokyo
リトル東京
Düsseldorf · デュッセルドルフ
www.tokyodorf.com
Little Tokyo
リトル東京
アルト
Altbier
アルト
Altbier
アルト
Altbier
アルト
Little Tokyo
リトル東京
Düsseldorf · デュッセルドルフ
www.tokyodorf.com

エビ
アルト

NEWS
EVENTS
ORTE
Straßenfest auf der Immermannstraße

Pompoms

Design Agency • **Serious Studio**

Pompoms is a fast casual restaurant that cooks up fresh and delicious fries in an old-fashioned way. French fries have always been the ultimate comfort food, and Serious Studio's strategy for this brand was to create a look that evokes a fun obsession with this classic snack. The fry obsession applies even down to the logo. It features a hedgehog-inspired creature made of fries brought to life. The look of the brand was designed to be loose, to feel good and to convey an imperfect charm.

LOGO

POMPOMS

pretty fly for a double fry

FONT · Helvetica

ABCDEFGHIJKLM
NOPQRSTUVWXYZ
abcdefghijklm
nopqrstuvwxyz
1234567890

COLOR

C0 M93 Y76 K0

C2 M9 Y100 K0

C1 M2 Y18 K0

GRAPHIC

THE ALL SEEING FRY
CUT & FRIED ON SIGHT
HERE'S A TIP:
FROM SCRATCH
YES, WE MAKE IT
HAVE SOME DIP
WORKS LIKE MAGIC!
PRETTY FLY
POMPOMS
FOR A DOUBLE FRY
A SIZE FOR ALL
SMALLIN'
TALLIN'
BALLIN'
90
110
130
THE SAUCE IS THE BOSS
ADD
Garlic Mayonnaise
Street Barbecue Sauce
Sate Sauce
Banana Ketchup
Homemade Ketchup
Adobo Gravy
POWDER POWER
Parmesan and herbs
Furikake
Chili
Sour Cream and onion
TOP OF THE TOPS
Raclette Cheese
Mushroom Cream
Pork Floss with Butter
FRYING SAUCER FOUND
POTATOES
LOCALLY SOURCED
TOTALLY SCORES!
THE SAUCE IS
THE BOSS.
Pretty fly
for a
double fry.

POMPOMS
THE SAUCE IS
THE BOSS.

POMPOMS
LOCALLY SOURCED
TOTALLY SCORES!
Pretty fly
for a
double fry.
FRYING SAUCER FOUND
"THE FRIES WERE PAIRED WITH OUT OF THIS WORLD, HANDMADE SAUCES, I SWEAR!"
THE SAUCE IS
THE BOSS.
HERE'S A TIP:
HAVE SOME DIP
FIRST FRY
POTATOES
LOCALLY SOURCED
TOTALLY SCORES!
POMPOMS
Pretty fly

907470
FRYING SAUCER FOUND
POMPOMS
SAUCER SAUCER SAUCER
THE SAUCE IS THE BOSS
TRIPPING THE DIPPING
IT WAS LOVE AT FIRST FRY
POTATOES
Pretty fly for a

from scratch.
FRIES TO MEET YOU.
JULIEN AGOSTA
FOUNDING PARTNER
POMPOMS
Pretty fly for a double fry
POTATOES
LOCALLY SOURCED
TOTALLY SCORES!
are cut &

POMPOMS
Cash only

POMPOMS
LIVE THE FRYLAND LIFESTYLE
POMPOMS
pretty fly for a double fry

Golden Ring of Russia

Design • **Sorokina Natalia**

The Golden Ring of Russia is a famous ring of cities with ancient monuments of history and culture. They do not form a perfect circle but numerous enclosed forms. This variability and diversity form the basis of the brand identity: *For each person—each ring.* The uniqueness of Russian culture lies in its contrast, as in its churches, which are chaste and white on the outside and rich with colors inside. This was taken into consideration during the search for the color concept of the identity. The chosen logotype is a simple logo for tourists that incorporates icons symbolizing some of the individual cities.

LOGO

ЗОЛОТОЕ
КОЛЬЦО
РОССИИ

FONT · Geometria

ABCDEFGHIJKLM
NOPQRSTUVWXYZ
abcdefghijklm
nopqrstuvwxyz
1234567890

COLOR

C93 M75 Y0 K0

C0 M93 Y76 K0

C20 M33 Y100 K7

C0 M0 Y0 K100

GRAPHIC

ЗОЛОТОЕ КОЛЬЦО РОССИИ
РОСТОВ
ЗОЛОТОЕ КОЛЬЦО РОССИИ
ЯРОСЛАВЛЬ

ЗОЛОТОЕ КОЛЬЦО РОССИИ
ЯРОСЛАВЛЬ
Дата
12 марта, суббота
Адрес
Сквер на улице Андропова
Программа
Выступление творческих коллективов Ярославской области и Областного Дома народного творчества. Игра «За блинами я пойду», веселая конкурсная программа
1234567890

Voice: Speech and Voice Training

Design Agency • **ICARUS**
Client • **Verena Covi**

Speech and voice training has been developed for people who want to optimize their speech and voice skills. ICARUS's goal was to make voice and language training as approachable as possible. Their idea was to visualize sound, so they recorded the individual letters of the brand name with an audio program and simplified the resulting waveforms. The visualization of audio waves, which embodies the versatility of pronunciation and intonation, forms the basis of this corporate identity. In their simplified form, these waves create a dynamic image. A world of vibrant colors with purple and orange hues gives Verena Covi's speech and voice training business a distinct and surprising look. The diversity of language is thus expressed through 50 different variants of the same motif on the business cards.

LOGO

FONT • Averta

ABCDEFGHIJKLM
NOPQRSTUVWXYZ
abcdefghijklm
nopqrstuvwxyz
1234567890

COLOR

- C0 M84 Y77 K0
- C88 100 Y5 K0
- C0 M0 Y0 K100

GRAPHIC

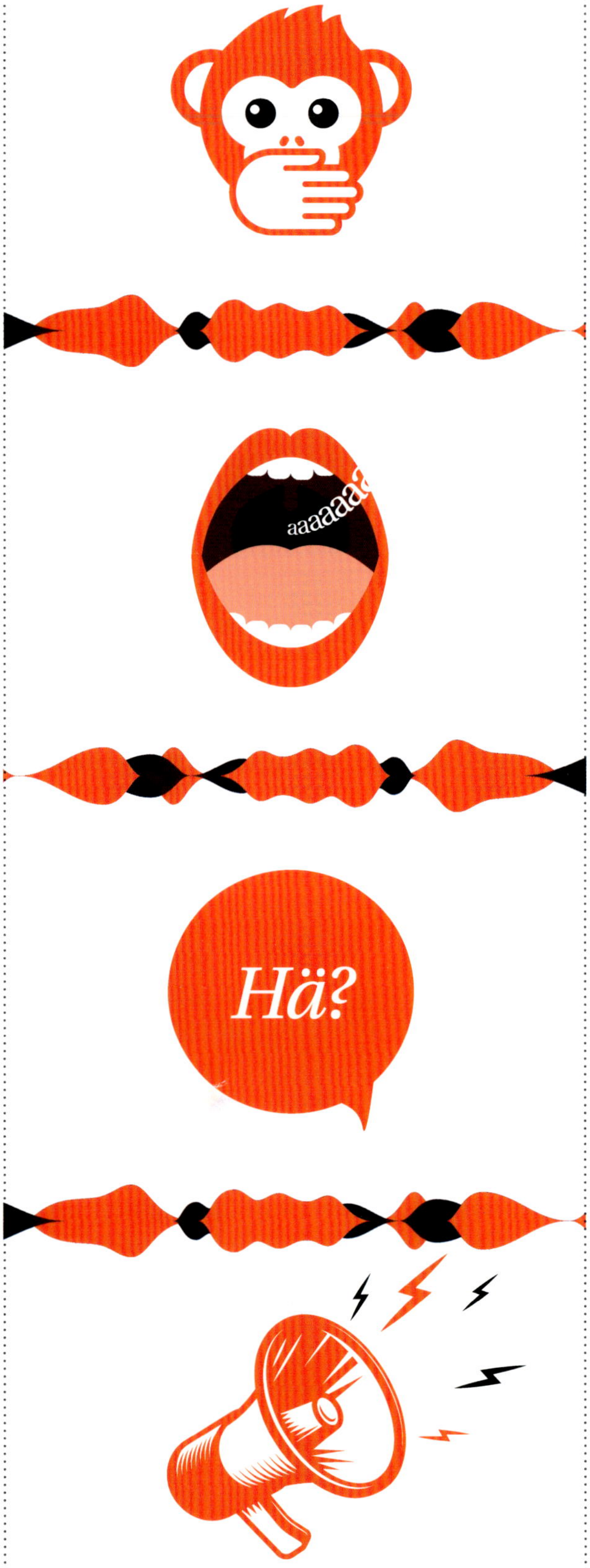

[ʔeː]
Verena
Covi MBA
+43(0)699 13100400
info@sprechtechnik.at
sprechtechnik.at
[iː]

Im täglichen »business«
kann der Klang Ihrer Stimme
Berge versetzen.
Sprechen wir darüber.
[ˈbɪznəs]
www.sprechtechnik.at

Wściekła Rybka

Design Agency • **The Goort**
Art Direction • **Aleksandr Gusakov**
Client • **Wściekła Rybka gastro bar**
Photography • **Aleksandr Gusakov**

The identity project of this gastro bar started long before the interior designing began. During the first appointment with the client, The Goort was tasked with the continuation of the project. The agency elaborated upon the name, which translates from the Polish as "crazy fish." This image provided the basis for the whole corporate identity. The typographic style reminds people of the Polish visual culture. Surreal illustrations with geometric shapes were chosen for the corporate identity, while the subdued tone of dark red completes the classical color combination.

LOGO

WŚCIEKŁA
RYBKA
GASTRO BAR

FONT • Biko

ABCDEFGHIJKLM
NOPQRSTUVWXYZ
abcdefghijklm
nopqrstuvwxyz
1234567890

COLOR

C15 M100 Y90 K10
C0 M0 Y0 K0
C0 M0 Y0 K100

GRAPHIC

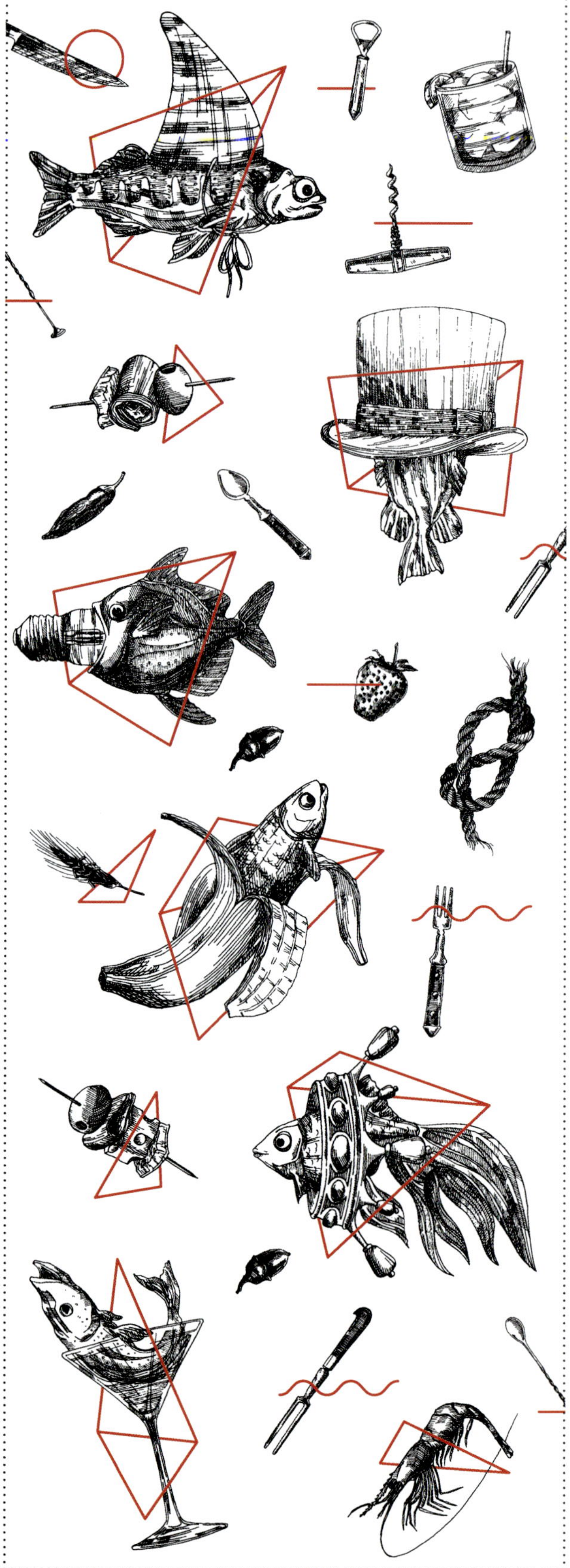

WŚCIEKŁA
RYBKA
Nowogrodzka 22
Warszawa
+4 822 127-72-18

WŚCIEKŁA
RYBKA
BLACK
BERRY
CACAO
CHOIX

BLACK
BERRY
Liqueur
POLMOS. LIKIER JEŻYNOWY
29% — 50 ML

TENTH // 25
Goat Cheese, Shaved Asparagus,
Chive-Infused Oil
SWEETS
ELEVENTH // 15
Labneh, Grapes, Almonds
TWELFTH // 20
Maple Syrup, Flaxseeds, Pecans
THIRTEENTH // 18
Apples, Honey, Goat Cheese,
Pomegranate Seeds, Walnut
NORWEGIAN // 25
Bourbon, Ginger, Raspberry,
Passion Fruit and Cinnamon
LABRADOR // 23
Gin on tea, Maple syrup, Lemon
FALKLAND // 24
Vodka, Pineapple, Lemon,
Passion fruit, Coconut, Basil
IRMINGER // 20
Gin, Coconut, Lime, Blueberry
GULF STREAM // 22
Three kinds of rum, Falernum,
Lime, Pineapple, Orange
EL NIÑO // 19
Gin on tea, Aperol, Martini
MINDANAO // 23
Vodka on buckwheat, Ginger,
Lemon, Honey
KUROSHIO // 25
Vodka, Celery, Tabasco, Lemon,
Tomato juice
DRINKS
WATER // 12
sparkling / still
COCA-COLA // 15
SCHWEPPES // 15
FRESH SQUEEZED
JUICE // 20
orange, grapefruit, apple, carrot, celery
COFFEE
AND TEA
COFFEE
ESPRESSO // 15
DOPPIO // 18
WŚCIEKŁA
RYBKA
GASTRO

Ila Barú

Design Agency • **Estudio Yeyé**
Art Direction • **Orlando Portillo**
Photography • **Raúl Villalobos**

Ila Barú is a nutrition center with an organic market and juice bar. Estudio Yeyé's objective was to capture the spirit of nature that lies within plants, vegetables, and fruits. With detailed photography, the designers reveal the hidden worlds inside food, creating a perfect canvas to develop a branding identity.

LOGO

FONT · Apercu Mono

ABCDEFGHIJKLM
NOPQRSTUVWXYZ
abcdefghijklm
nopqrstuvwxyz
1234567890

COLOR

C0 M0 Y0 K100 C1 M20 Y42 K0

GRAPHIC

Dosis de sabiduría
03
Mucho trato, poco plato, gasta la suela de tu zapato.
Oscar Legarreta

Dosis de sabiduría
02
La mejor farmacia: tus alimentos.
Oscar Legarreta
Sabiduría en el comer

Matamores

Design Agency • **Estudio Yeyé**
Art Direction • **Orlando Portillo**
Photography • **Raúl Villalobos**

Matamores goes beyond trendy mezcal offerings. With a handmade bottle and limited and exquisite production, the brand transforms this craft drink into a true work of art. Estudio Yeyé used the figure of *Kauymali*, from the mythology of the Huichol people of Mexico. The image reinterprets one of the representative figures of the Huichol culture within a simple and sophisticated language, preserving the mystery of the Huichol culture and bottling its mysticism.

LOGO

MATAMORES

FONT · Apercu Mono

ABCDEFGHIJKLM
NOPQRSTUVWXYZ
abcdefghijklm
nopqrstuvwxyz
1234567890

COLOR

C23 M67 Y93 K11 C0 M0 Y0 K100

GRAPHIC

EL SABOR
DE LOS
SAGUAROS
Y LAS
NUBES

TAMO

TAMO

Casa Olmo

Design Agency • **Estudio Nuar**
Art Direction • **Santiago Olguin**
Architecture • **Hitzig Militello Arquitectos**
Illustration • **Stock Images**
Photography • **Esteban Lobo**

Casa Olmo is a pub located in Ushuaia, Argentina, known by tourists as "the city at the end of the world." In order to preserve the spirit of the place and its magic, Estudio Nuar and the architects decided to play with the wealth of imaginings associated with this region, with special reference to the fantastic marine world of Jules Vernes and the discoveries of Darwin. Their creative proposal was based on improving original attributes of the pub through a contemporary design approach. Estudio Nuar created a visual identity that elegantly communicates brand values without competing with the illustrated interior design. The typographic selection maintains a classic tone with modern details. The illustrations of the underwater magical world appear on different pieces such as the menu and personal cards, but in a simple and subtle way.

LOGO

Casa Ølmõ
BAR DE AGUAS SALVAJES

FONT • PlayfairDisplay

ABCDEFGHIJKLM
NOPQRSTUVWXYZ
abcdefghijklm
nopqrstuvwxyz
1234567890

COLOR

C0 M0 Y0 K100

C8 M5 Y7 K20

GRAPHIC

Casa Ølmõ
BAR DE AGUAS SALVAJES
CAPE HORN
E-Mail
hola@casaolmoushuaia.com.ar
Facebook
Instagram
@casaolmo
ushuaia
Tel.
2901.42.2824
AV. SAN MARTÍN 87, USHUAIA, TIERRA DEL FUEGO

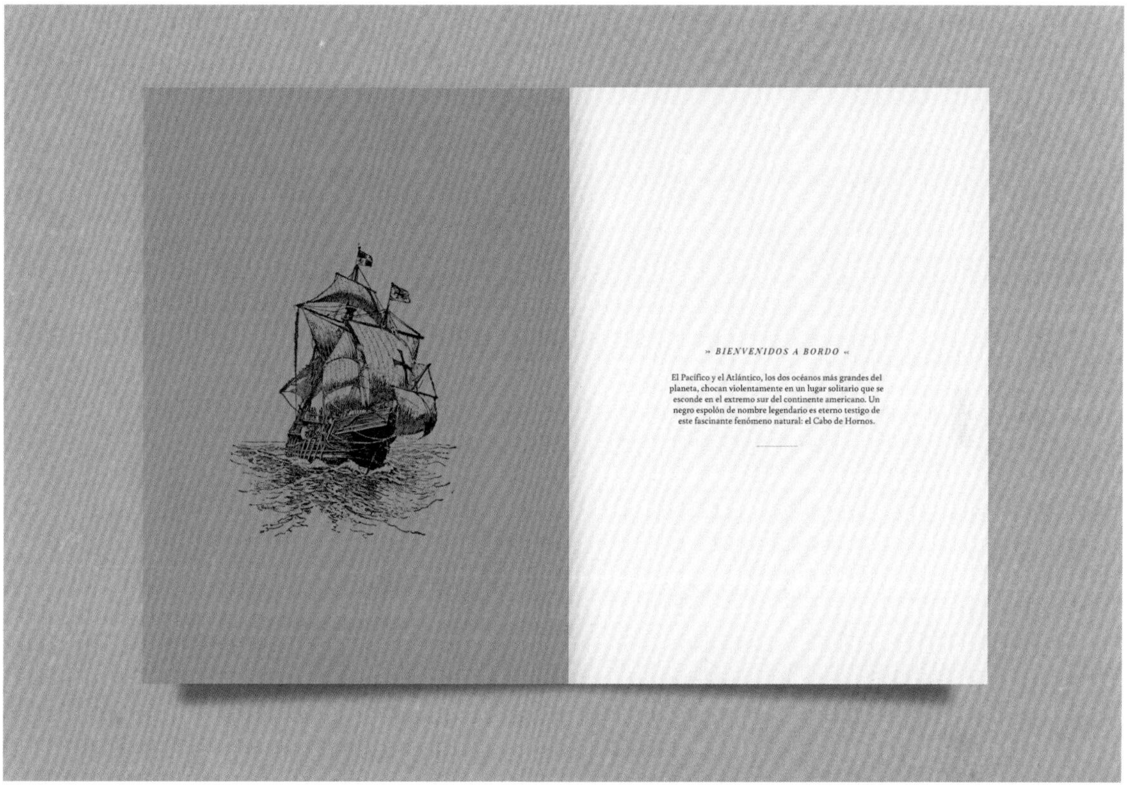

» BIENVENIDOS A BORDO «
El Pacífico y el Atlántico, los dos océanos más grandes del planeta, chocan violentamente en un lugar solitario que se esconde en el extremo sur del continente americano. Un negro espolón de nombre legendario es eterno testigo de este fascinante fenómeno natural: el Cabo de Hornos.

« Bebidas »
CERVEZAS
CAPE HORN TIRADA
Pinta » $ 20
Cerveza de elaboración artesanal
NEGRA
ROJA
y también
RUBIA
Jarra » $ 20
Presentada por Fuegian Beverage Co.
ANTARES HONEY
Argentina, Rubia Miel, Alc: 7,5 %, IBU: 22. 500 ml $ 20
ANTARES IMPERIAL STOUT
Argentina, Negra, Alc: 8,5 %. 500 ml $ 20
ANTARES KOLSCH
Argentina, Lager Extra, Alc: 5 %, IBU: 22. 500 ml $ 20
ANTARES PORTER
Argentina, Negra, Alc: 5,5 %. 500 ml $ 20
ANTARES SCOTCH
Argentina, Scotch Ale, Alc: 5,5 %, IBU: 18. 500 ml $ 20
ANTARES WINE
Argentina, Lager Extra, Alc: 10 %, IBU: 53. 500 ml $ 20
BEAGLE NEGRA
Argentina, Clásica Negra, Alc: 6,2 %, IBU: 21. 330 ml $ 20
BEAGLE ROJA
Argentina, Clásica Roja, Alc: 6,1 %, IBU: 24,5. 330 ml $ 20
BEAGLE RUBIA
Argentina, Clásica Rubia, Alc: 4,8 %, IBU: 20. 330 ml $ 20
CAPE HORN HONEY
Argentina, Rubia Miel, Alc: 7,2 %, IBU: 20. 500 ml $ 20
CAPE HORN NUT BROWN ALE
Argentina, rubia miel, Alc: 7,5 %, IBU: 22. 500 ml $ 20
CAPE HORN OATMEL STOUT
Argentina, Brown Ale, Alc: 7,2 %, IBU: 22. 500 ml $ 20
CAPE HORN PALE ALE
Argentina, Pale Ale, Alc: 4,8 %, IBU: 21. 500 ml $ 20

Casa Ølmõ
BAR DE AGUAS SALVAJES
>> LES DAMOS LA BIENVENIDA A BORDO <<
AV. SAN MARTÍN 87, USHUAIA, TIERRA DEL FUEGO
GOB. DELOQUI
AV. SAN MARTIN
AV. MAIPÚ
GODOY
RIVADAVIA
ANTÁRTIDA ARG.
YAGANES
AV. SAN MARTIN 87
CAPE HORN
CERVEZA DEL FIN DEL MUNDO
E-Mail
hola@casaolmoushuaia.com.ar
Facebook Instagram
@casaolmo ushuaia
Tel.
2901.42.2824
ABIERTO LUNES A DOMINGOS DE 17 A 4 HS

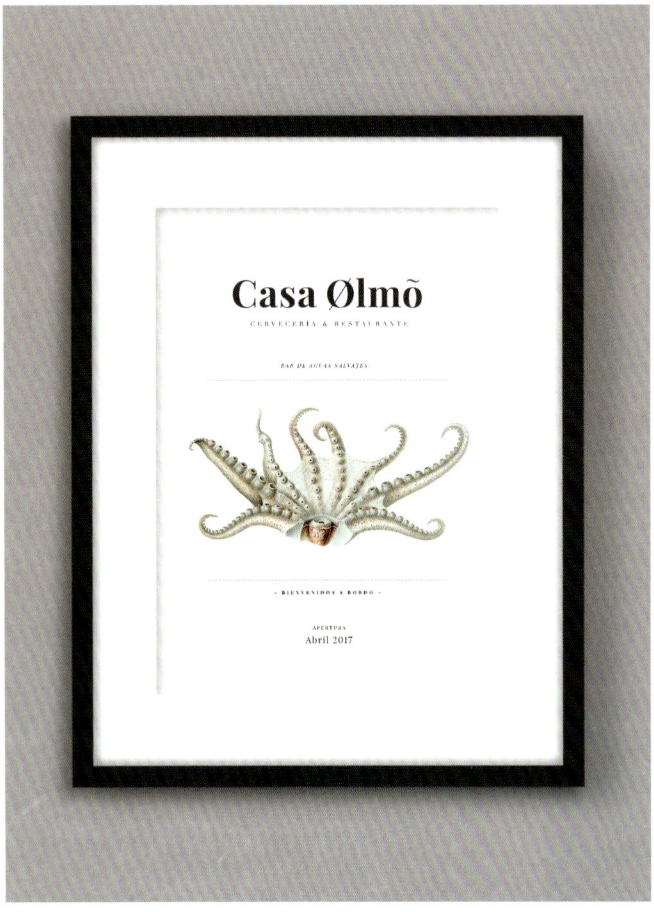
Casa Ølmõ
CERVECERÍA & RESTAURANTE
BAR DE AGUAS SALVAJES
~ BIENVENIDOS A BORDO ~
APERTURA
Abril 2017

Casa Ølmõ
CERVECERÍA & RESTAURANTE
1903
ABRE UN NUEVO BAR EN UNA CASA HISTÓRICA
2017
19 hs 5/04/17
LES DAMOS LA BIENVENIDA A BORDO
COMIDA
COCKTAILS
CERVEZA
SIÉNTANSE COMO EN SU CASA

Casa Ølmõ
Bar de aguas salvajes
CAPE HORN®
WORLD'S SOUTHERNMOST BEER

Muuuu

Design • **Nadja Olić**

This project is a branding design for dairy products. The logo and the name come from the sound that cows make and its shape represents the udder of a cow. Visual identity is a combination of modern pure typography and vibrant colored illustrations consisting of simple geometric shapes. The design was applied to bottles and ceramic mugs, blending rustic handmade ceramics and a modern minimalist design. This work came from the goal to create modern and unusual packaging designs for the products that people use in everyday life, with an emphasis on innovative design.

LOGO

( )
MUUUU

FONT · Orator Std

ABCDEFGHIJKLM
NOPQRSTUVWXYZ
ABCDEFGHIJKLM
NOPQRSTUVWXYZ
1234567890

COLOR

C12 M56 Y87 K0
C95 M92 Y26 K0
C30 M9 Y40 K0
C13 M86 Y100 K4

GRAPHIC

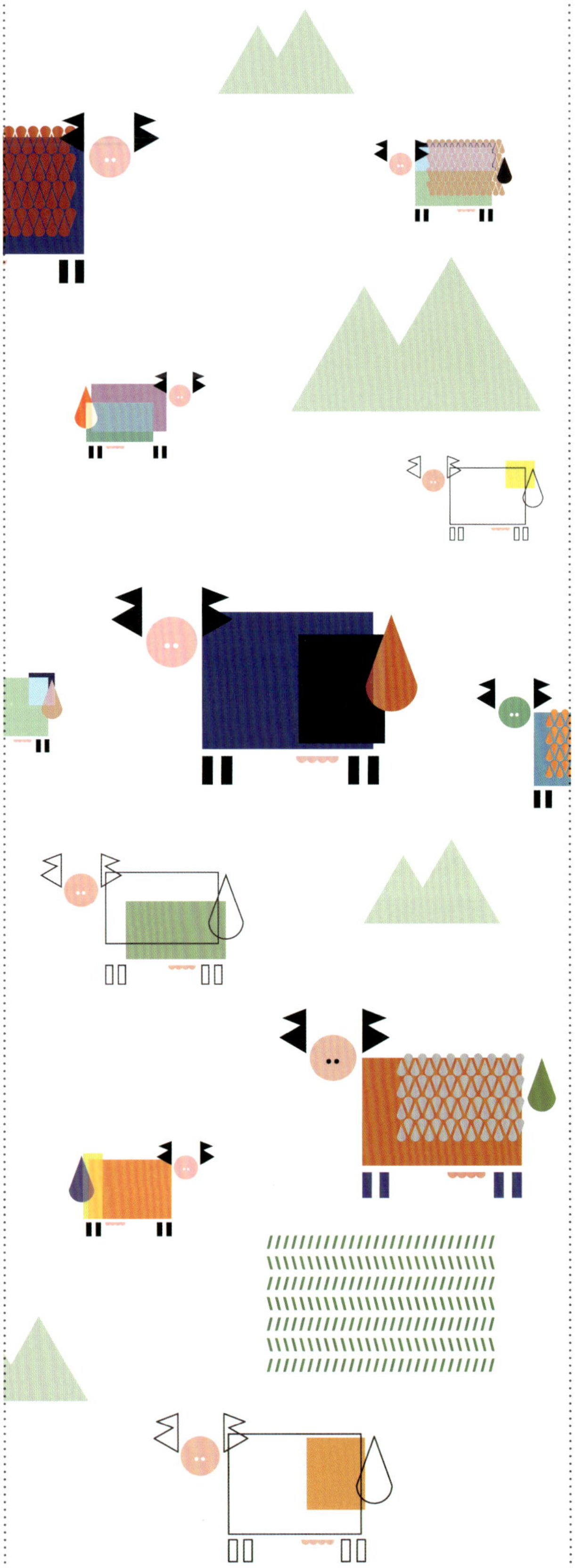

MLECNI
PROIZVOD
JOGURT

KISELO
MLEKCE
COKOLADNO
MLEKCE
KAJMAKCI
PAVLAKICA

MLECNI
PROIZVOD
JOGURT
SVAKOG DANA
MLEKARICA
DONOSI VAM
NOVU SVEZU
FLASU
ORGANIC

Niditas

Design Agency • Mubien
Art Direction • David Mubien
Design • David Mubien
Photography • Víctor Mubien, Sergio Cuevas

Niditas is an equestrian hotel specializing in romantic surprises. Mubien worked on the naming and the visual identity and developed the business concept with the owners. They crafted the stationery in their workshop and collaborated with Pardo Interior on the decoration and signage of the building.

LOGO

NIDITAS

FONT · Rufina

ABCDEFGHIJKLM
NOPQRSTUVWXYZ
abcdefghijklm
nopqrstuvwxyz
1234567890

COLOR

C0 M0 Y0 K100

C51 M40 Y39 K20

GRAPHIC

Una experiencia inolvidable
NIDITAS
Hay algo especial para ti en el interior...
Octavio Martínez
NIDITAS

Stage 12: Hotel by Penz

Design Agency • **ICARUS**
Client • **Family Penz**
Photography • **Günther Egger**

Stage 12 is a modern city hotel in the center of Innsbruck, Austria. The new identity aims to convey both visually and verbally the hotel's special location on one of Innsbruck's main shopping streets, as well as its international flair. The idea was to create a hotel branding that has never been seen in Innsbruck before. Instead of the typical Tyrolean clichés and local tourism messages, ICARUS went for a fresh design. Stylish illustrations and eye-catching color combinations replaced photos already seen a thousand times. ICARUS created a feel of genuine authenticity far away from shiny brochures and menu covers made of artificial leather. The written messages speak a young language—delivered with a subtle nod and a wink.

LOGO

STAGE12

FONT • Biotif

ABCDEFGHIJKLM
NOPQRSTUVWXYZ
abcdefghijklm
nopqrstuvwxyz
1234567890

COLOR

C20 M25 Y70 K0
C97 M5 Y41 K24
C0 M50 Y45 K0

GRAPHIC

KOSTA
STAGE12
HOTEL BY PENZ
Daniel Penz
Stage 12 Hotel GmbH
Maria-Theresien-Straße 12
6020 Innsbruck, Austria
daniel.penz@stage12.at
+43.699.10087550
STAGE12
HOTEL BY PENZ

Do not make my room great again.
STAGE12
Make my room great again.
STAGE12

DRINK THIS OR LEAVE.
(OHNE)
KAFF(T)EE
BIER
WEINE & CO.
12 DRINKS 24/7
HOCHPROZENTIG

STAGE
HOMEMADE
JAM

SODA

SAUNA

601--607
6th

STAGE12 HOTEL
STAGE12
HOTEL BY PENZ

Hokkaidon

Design Agency • **A Work of Substance**
Client • **1957 & Co. Restaurant Group**
Photography • **Vita Mak**

A unique take on a traditional motif, Hokkaidon's graphic expression is a disruption of the tranquil pattern of *seigaiha*, the instantly recognizable blue rolling waves. The energy of the sea-to-table dishes unravels on the murals as an array of eclectic seafood, breaking through the blue and white boundaries of the ocean and adding renewed vigor to this piece of Japanese heritage. Rice, the foundation of Japanese food and culture, is at the core of the logo, creating a pure and distinct brand that reflects the essence of *chirashi*.

LOGO

FONT · Hind

ABCDEFGHIJKLM
NOPQRSTUVWXYZ
abcdefghijklm
nopqrstuvwxyz
1234567890

COLOR

C97 M88 Y37 K30

C0 M0 Y0 K0

GRAPHIC

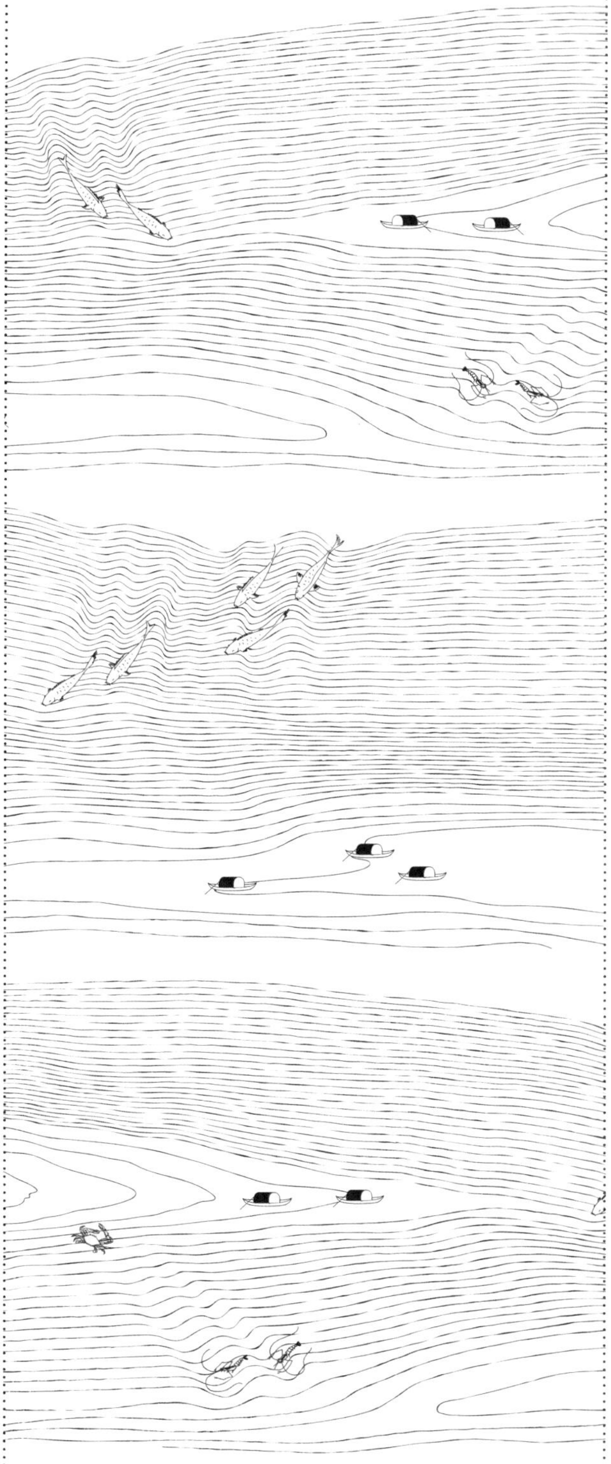

HOKKAIDON
北海丼
T 2577 0828 F 2577 0928
enquiry@hokkaidon.com.hk
hokkaidon.com.hk

FOOD
BEVERAGE

HOKKAIDON

HOKKAIDON
北海丼

Pica Pica Concept Store

Design Agency • we are two
Art Direction • we are two
Design • we are two
Photography • Grigoris Leontiades

Pica Pica Concept Store is a play space—a cafe with a shop that encourages socialization and creativity in children and strengthens their relationship with their parents. The name is inspired by the Latin name of the magpie. Mainly focused on children, we are two created a unique, colorful and customizable corporate identity, inspired by the children's game of wooden blocks. By converting the blocks into letters, the agency created the graphics of the venue while also expressing the logo and the entire design of the corporate identity, keeping the same pattern in every new application.

LOGO

PICA PICA
concept store

FONT · Custom Font

COLOR

C0 M12 Y92 K0
C0 M46 Y14 K0
C38 M3 Y45 K7
C81 M55 Y0 K0

GRAPHIC

hAPPY b-DAY
DREAM biG
STAND TALL
JOY IS hOME MADE
hELLO SUN ShiNE
hAVE FUN
hAPPY b-DAY
STAND TALL
hELLO SUN ShiNE

PiCA PiCA

PRiCE LiST
PiCA PiCA

PICAPICA
ENJOY

Kakigōri

Design Agency • **LIE DESIGN & ART DIRECTION**
Art Direction • **Driv Loo, Magdalene Wong**
Design • **Magdalene Wong**
Client • **Kakigōori**
Photography • **Heartpatrick**

Kakigōri was the first Japanese shaved-ice dessert bar in Kuala Lumpur. LIE created a fictional character as the main character and logo for the brand—Yuki, a lady made of snow yet fascinated by the tropical world. As much as she enjoys the hot weather, her body can't stand the heat. In order to prevent herself from melting, she eats ice.

LOGO

KAKI
GŌRI

FONT • Akzidenz-Grotesk

ABCDEFGHIJKLM
NOPQRSTUVWXYZ
abcdefghijklm
nopqrstuvwxyz
1234567890

COLOR

C69 M0 Y26 K0

GRAPHIC

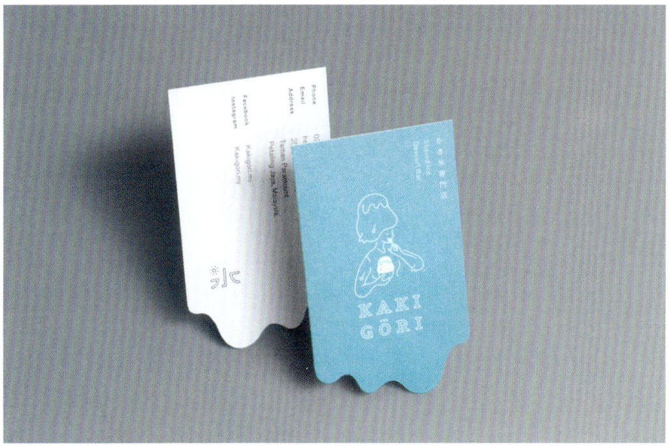
KAKI
GŌRI

To & Do

Design Agency • LIE DESIGN & ART DIRECTION
Art Direction • Driv Loo
Design • Annabell Heng
Illustration • Driv Loo, Annabell Heng

To & Do Pet Home is named after the owner's dog, "Todo." LIE added the ampersand (&) in the middle of the logotype to symbolize the nose and mouth of a dog, making the logotype a character on its own.

LOGO

FONT · Effra

ABCDEFGHIJKLM
NOPQRSTUVWXYZ
abcdefghijklm
nopqrstuvwxyz
1234567890

COLOR

C100 M100 Y100 K100

C0 M0 Y0 K0

GRAPHIC

to&do
FANNY LIM
Director
016 521 4463
To & Do Pet Home
18, Jalan SS2/55,
Selangor DE, Malaysia
T 03 78653354
FB fb.com/todopethom

TUKATA

Creative Direction • Tyodi Hyojin Lee
Illustration • Hayoung Jung
Photography • Soonjeong Yoo

The brand identity of TUKATA seeks to blend interest with longevity. The design choices reflect the handmade brand's characteristics with its own handwritten typeface and suggest an authentic attitude with the use of monotone color.

LOGO

TUKATA®

FONT · TUKATA Regular

All products are handmade for your new perspective

COLOR

CO MO YO KO

CO MO YO K100

GRAPHIC

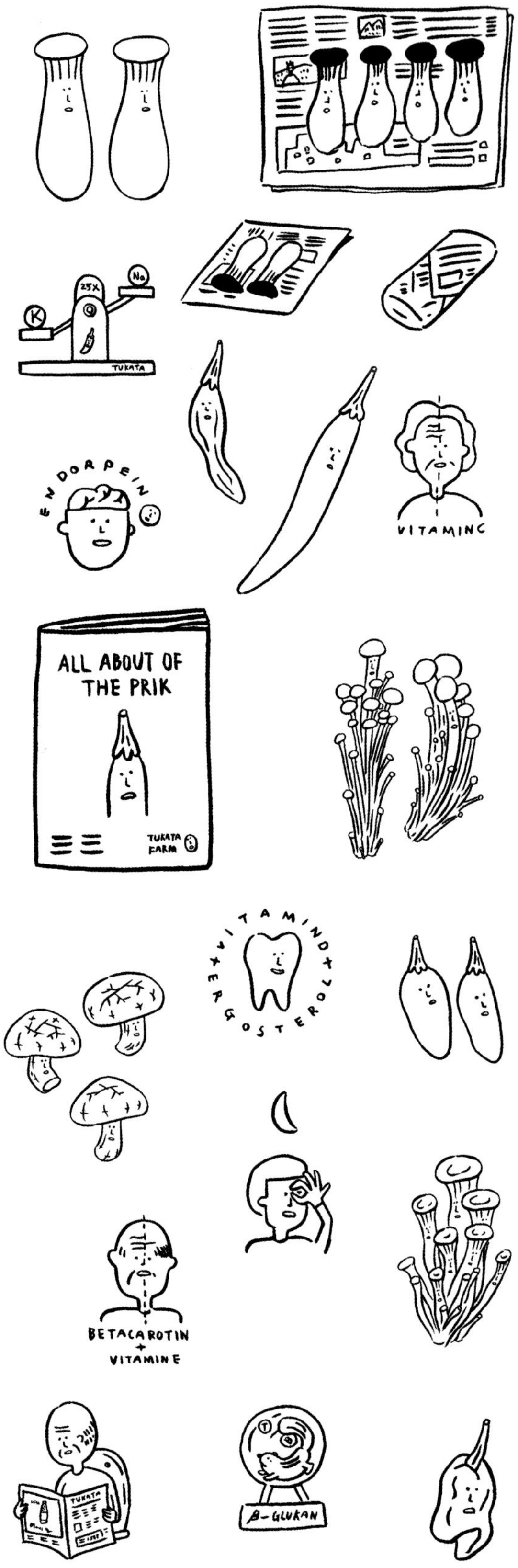

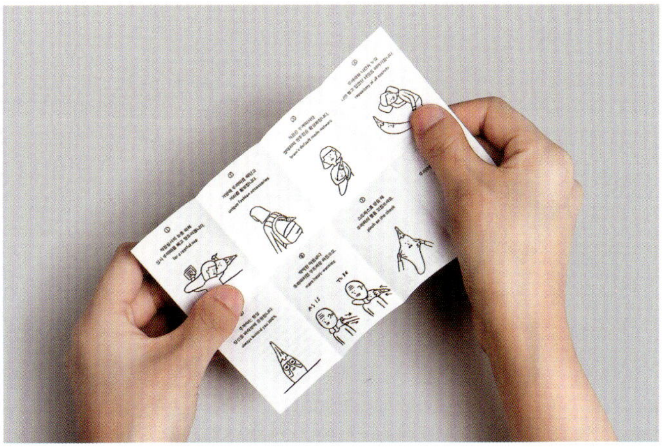

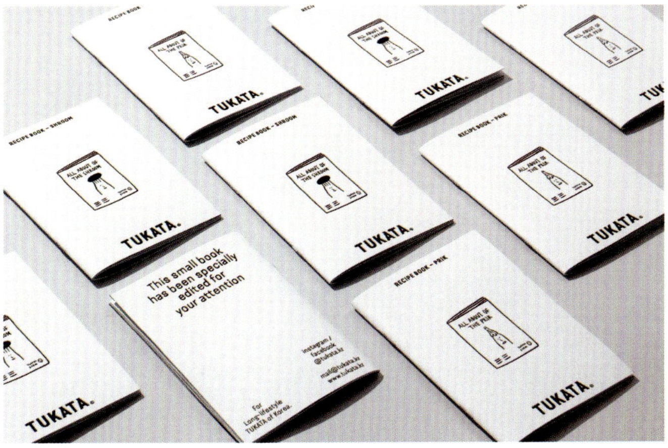
TUKATA.
This small book has been specially edited for your attention
TUKATA.

TUKATA.
TUKATA.

for
ng-lifest
TUKATA®

All products
are handmade for
your new perspective
Long-lifestyle
TUKATA of Korea.
Head is from polyester 63%, rayon 33%
and spandex 4%, Body is made from polyester
90%, rayon 10% and babylon ball fiber

TUKATA prik green (small size) ①premium fabric / ②terry-towel cotton
①Head is made from polyester 63%, rayon 33%and spandex 4%. Body is made from polyester 90%, rayon 10% and babylon ball fiber. ②Head & Body is made from terry towel-cotton85%, polyester 15% and babylon ball fiber.
All products are handmade for your new perspective. Long-lifestyle, TUKATA of Korea.
instagram / facebook @tukata.kr mail@tukata.kr

Buffy

Design Agency • Pentagram
Art Direction • Natasha Jen
Design • Natasha Jen, Joseph Han, Jang Hyun Han, Ena Yun

Light as a cloud, temperature-regulating, and vegan-friendly, Buffy is the world's most comfortable and kindest duvet. Pentagram developed brand identity, positioning, messaging and packaging for the new product, highlighting its softness and innovative technology. Visually, a comforter is not the most interesting object, so the challenge for the designers was to create a graphic personality that captures the Buffy experience. Buffy's playful personality is expressed in the graphic identity, which is warm, outgoing and modern.

LOGO

Buffy

FONT Cooper

ABCDEFGHIJKLM
NOPQRSTUVWXYZ
abcdefghijklm
nopqrstuvwxyz
1234567890

COLOR

C44 M0 Y31 K0
C25 M12 Y0 K0
C4 M20 Y7 K0

GRAPHIC

Time for
Sweet Dreams
Buffy
Buffy
Buffy

YOU
DID IT

Resting Buffy Face
Buffy
Buffy
Buffy

Buffy

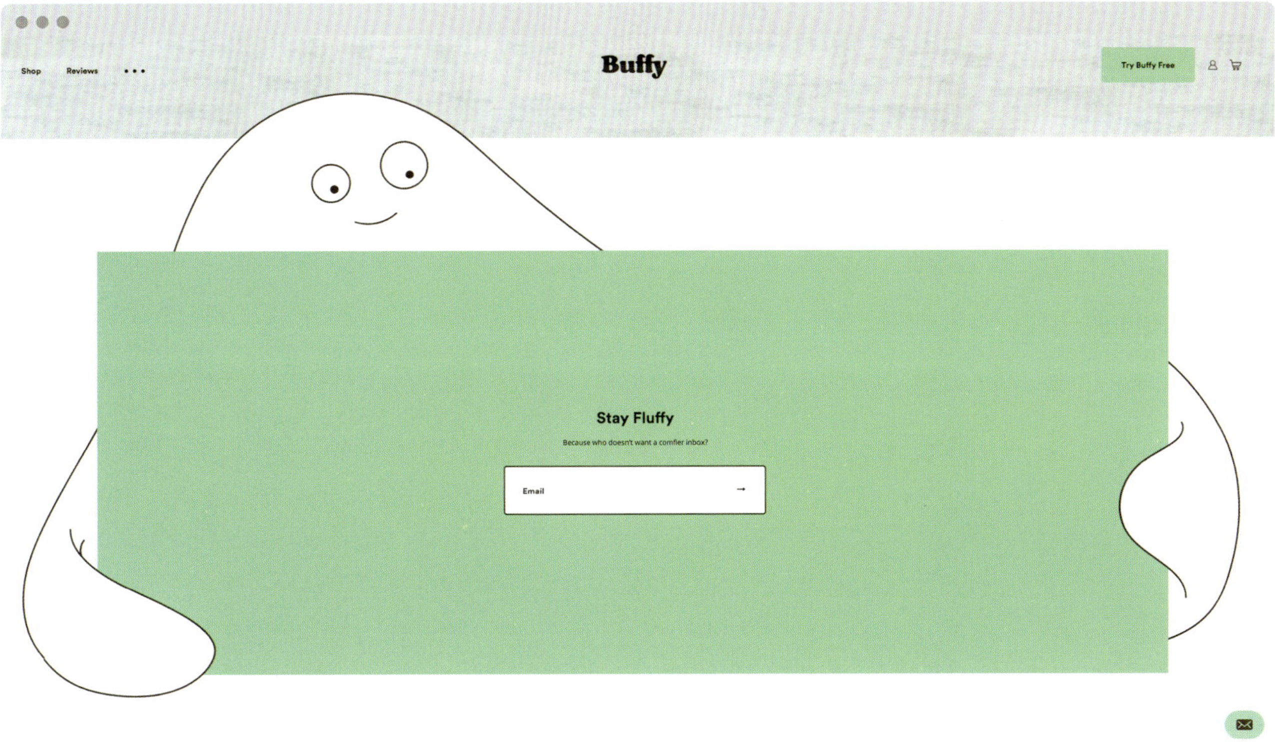
Shop
Reviews
Buffy
Try Buffy Free
Stay Fluffy
Because who doesn't want a comfier inbox?
Email

Xeom

Design Agency • **Hue Studio**
Creative Direction • **Vian Risanto**
Design • **Vian Risanto, Kumiko Michishita**
Client • **Xeom**
Illustration • **Vian Risanto**
Photography • **Jave Hooni**

Xeoms are Vietnam's ubiquitous motorcycle taxis. The drivers of Xeoms always know where to find the best food. You can find them scarfing a steaming bowl of pho and downing beers with their mates while playing *baucua ca cop*, a Vietnamese dice game. Drawing inspiration from the game, Hue Studio created a loud, brave and edgy brand identity for this Vietnamese street food joint by using meticulously hand-written letters and applying the elements from the game: cow, chicken, prawn, crab, fish, and wine.

LOGO

FONT · Custom Font

ALL WORK NO BREAK

COLOR

C0 M90 Y86 K0
C55 M0 Y40 K0
C10 M0 Y53 K0
C0 M0 Y0 K100

GRAPHIC

2 GRILLED
NEM NƯỚNG
DOUBLE OR NOTHING
BÒ LÁ LỐT
SKEWERS

CRISPY
BÁNH XÈO
SO GOOD!
VIETNAMESE PANCAKE

ĂN CHƠI
TO SHARE
CRUNCHY SPRING ROLLS
Prawn chicken or vegie 6pc 9
STREET STICKS
2 Grilled pork skewers 7.8
2 Grilled beef betel leaf skewers 7.8
2 SEXY ROLLS
Classic pork/prawn 6.5
Lemongrass chicken/beef 6.5
Tofu & avocado 6
Soft shell crab 7
Salmon & avocado 7
Smoke duck 7
SOMETHING GREEN
Poached chicken coleslaw 14.5
Tender beef coleslaw 14.5
Pork & prawn coleslaw 14.5
Crispy tofu coleslaw 13
NƯỚC UỐNG
DRINKS
BOOZE
VB 5.5
Bia Hanoi 7.5
Saigon 333 7.5
Tiger 7.5
Singha 7.5
Lychee Cider 8.5
FIZZY/JUICE/SMOOTHIE/COFFEE
Coke/Diet/Fanta/Sprite 3
Lemon ice tea w/ lychee 5.5
Fresh young coconut 5.5
Avocado smoothie 5.5
Vietnamese ice coffee 4
SPARKLING
San Pietro Sparkling Brut, Mornington VIC 8.5/42
WHITE WINES
Mount Vernon Sauvignon Blanc, Marlborough NZ 8.5/38
Quartier Pinot Gris, Mornington VIC 9/42
RED WINES
Bellvale Pinot Noir, Gippsland VIC 9/42
Xanadu NOK Shiraz, Maragret River WA 8/36
MÓN CHÍNH
BIT MORE
NOODLE SOUP PHO REAL
Tender beef or chicken 11
Tender beef & beef meat balls 12
Mushrooms & tofu 11
Combination: beef/brisket/tripe/beef ball/tendon/young egg yolk 13
VERMICELLI NOODLE/SALAD
Grilled chicken & spring rolls 13
Grilled pork & spring rolls 13
Beef lemongrass & spring rolls 13
Tofu, veggies & spring rolls 13
Crispy soft shell crab 14
BBH SPICY BEEF NOODLE SOUP
Beef & pork 12
BROKEN RICE
Crispy chicken 12
Grilled lemongrass chicken 12
Grilled pork chop 12
Dice pepper beef 12
Wok tossed tofu & veggies 12
CRISPY VIETNAMESE PANCAKE
Combination pork & prawn 14.8
Vegetarian 14.8
TRÁNG MIỆNG
SWEETS
DESSERTS
Three colour desserts 5.4
PLEASE ASK FOR OUR DAILY SPECIALS.
YES! WE HAVE GLUTEN FREE OPTIONS JUST ASK ONE OF OUR LOVELY STAFF.
194 SMITH STREET COLLINGWOOD VICTORIA 3066 03-9417 6969
EAT@XEOM.COM.AU WWW.XEOM.COM.AU
XEOMSTREETFOOD
Viêt Street Food

Việt Street Food
xeôm

ALL WORK NO BREAK
2 GRILLED
NEM NƯỚNG
DOUBLE OR NOTHING
BÒ LÁ LỐT
SKEWERS
NO SMOKING
CRISPY
BÁNH XÈO
VIETNAMESE PANCAKE
CƠM TẤM

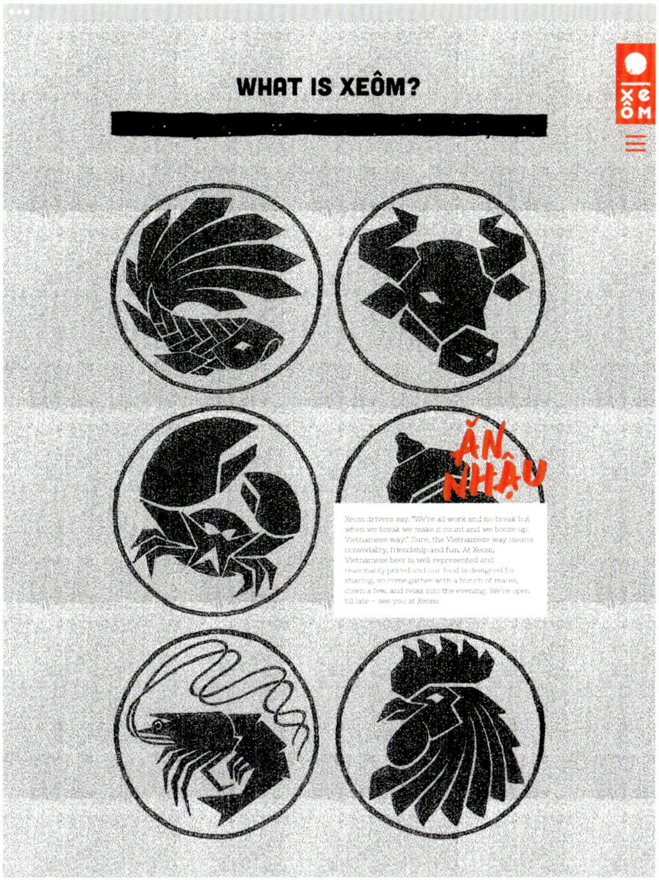
WHAT IS XEÔM?
ĂN NHẬU
Xeom drivers say, "We're all work and no break but when we break we make it count and we booze up. Vietnamese way!" Sure, the Vietnamese way means conviviality, friendship and fun. At Xeom, Vietnamese beer is well represented and reasonably priced and our food is designed for sharing, so come gather with a bunch of mates, down a few, and relax into the evening. We're open till late – see you at Xeom!

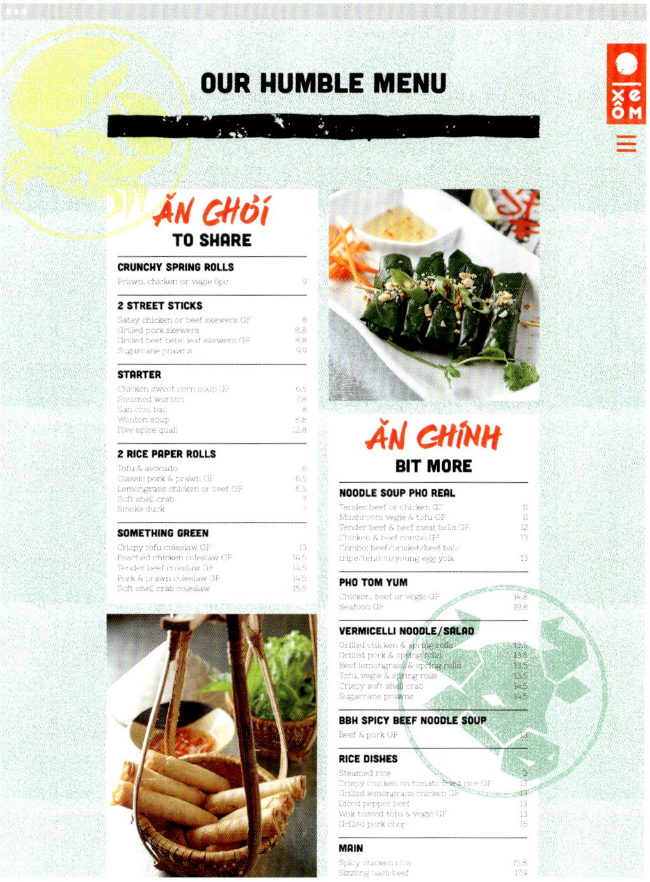
OUR HUMBLE MENU
ĂN CHƠI
TO SHARE
CRUNCHY SPRING ROLLS
Prawn, chicken or vegie 6pc 9
2 STREET STICKS
Satay chicken or beef skewers GF 8
Grilled pork skewers 8.8
Grilled beef betel leaf skewers GF 8.8
Sugarcane prawns 9.9
STARTER
Chicken sweet corn soup GF 6.5
Steamed wonton 7.8
San choi bao 8
Wonton soup 8.8
Five spice quail 12.8
2 RICE PAPER ROLLS
Tofu & avocado 6
Classic pork & prawn GF 6.5
Lemongrass chicken or beef GF 6.5
Soft shell crab 7
Smoke duck 7
SOMETHING GREEN
Crispy tofu coleslaw GF 13
Poached chicken coleslaw GF 14.5
Tender beef coleslaw GF 14.5
Pork & prawn coleslaw GF 14.5
Soft shell crab coleslaw 15.5
ĂN CHÍNH
BIT MORE
NOODLE SOUP PHO REAL
Tender beef or chicken GF 11
Mushroom vegie & tofu GF 11
Tender beef & beef meat balls GF 12
Chicken & beef combo GF 13
Combo: beef/brisket/beef ball/
tripe/tendon/young egg yolk 13
PHO TOM YUM
Chicken, beef or vegie GF 14.8
Seafood GF 19.8
VERMICELLI NOODLE/SALAD
Grilled chicken & spring rolls 13.5
Grilled pork & spring rolls 13.5
Beef lemongrass & spring rolls 13.5
Tofu, vegie & spring rolls 13.5
Crispy soft shell crab 14.5
Sugarcane prawns 14.5
BBH SPICY BEEF NOODLE SOUP
Beef & pork GF 13
RICE DISHES
Steamed rice 3
Crispy chicken on tomato fried rice GF 13
Grilled lemongrass chicken GF 13
Diced pepper beef 13
Wok tossed tofu & vegie GF 13
Grilled pork chop 15
MAIN
Spicy chicken ribs 15.8
Sizzling basil beef 17.9

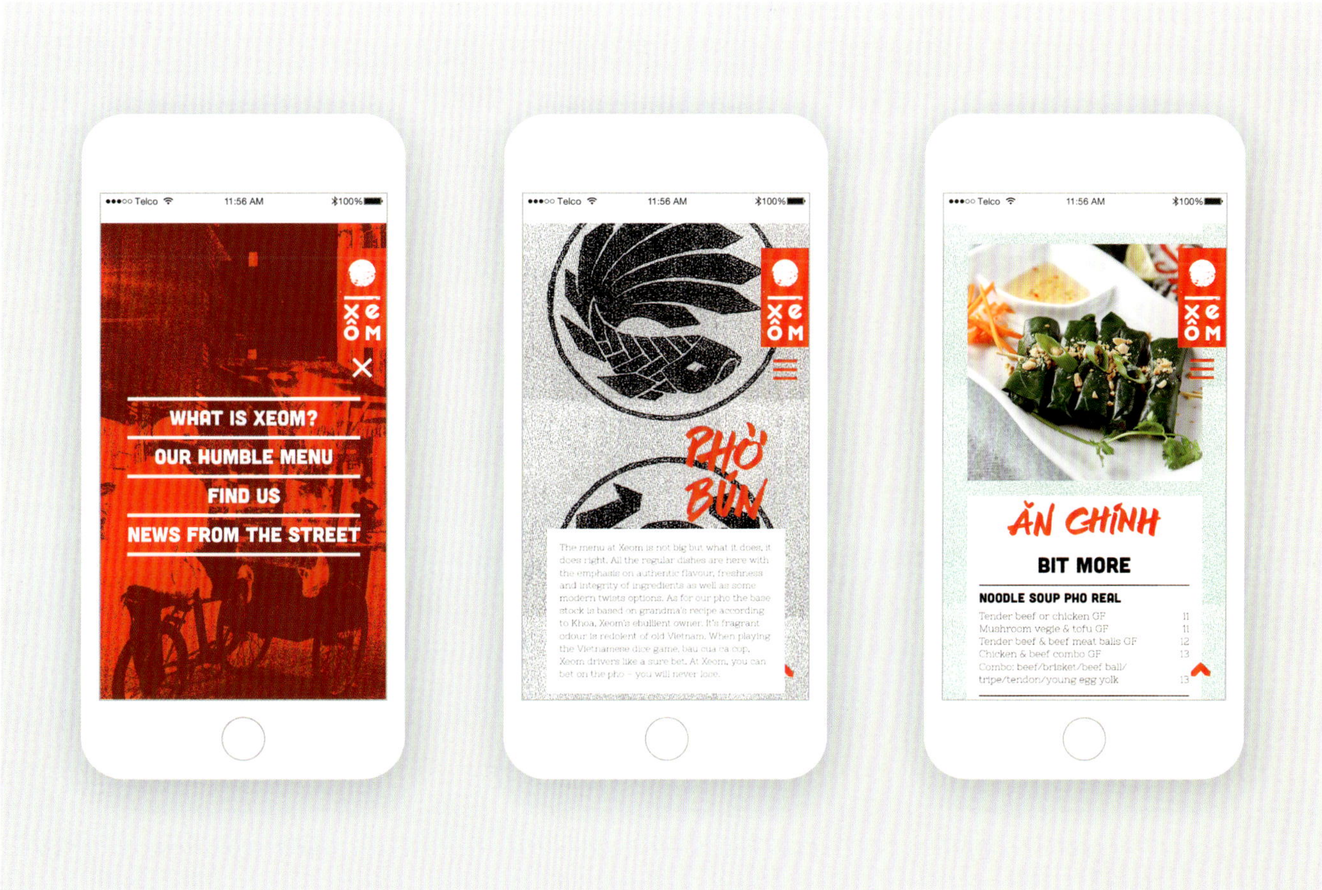
Telco 11:56 AM 100%
WHAT IS XEOM?
OUR HUMBLE MENU
FIND US
NEWS FROM THE STREET
Telco 11:56 AM 100%
PHỞ BÚN
The menu at Xeom is not big but what it does, it does right. All the regular dishes are here with the emphasis on authentic flavour, freshness and integrity of ingredients as well as some modern twists options. As for our pho the base stock is based on grandma's recipe according to Khoa, Xeom's ebullient owner. It's fragrant odour is redolent of old Vietnam. When playing the Vietnamese dice game, bau cua ca cup, Xeom drivers like a sure bet. At Xeom, you can bet on the pho – you will never lose.
Telco 11:56 AM 100%
ĂN CHÍNH
BIT MORE
NOODLE SOUP PHO REAL
Tender beef or chicken GF 11
Mushroom vegie & tofu GF 11
Tender beef & beef meat balls GF 12
Chicken & beef combo GF 13
Combo: beef/brisket/beef ball/
tripe/tendon/young egg yolk 13

Earlybird

Design Agency • **Necon**
Art Direction • **Krzysztof Nowak, Blazej Polkowski, Piotr Polus**
Design • **Monika Nowak**

Earlybird is a Zurich-based food delivery service focusing on fresh ingredients, healthy recipes, and a convenient ordering process. A delivery from Earlybird is supposed to be an energizing break from work. Thus, Necon designed a playful visual identity to emphasize this. Vibrant colors and fruit illustrations are at the core of Earlybird's identity system, and a library of hand-drawn ingredients lend themselves to the labels for new products, whether dishes or smoothies. A playful approach to composition allows Necon to easily create numerous branded collateral pieces and packages without restricting future creativity.

LOGO

earlybird

FONT · Apercu

ABCDEFGHIJKLM
NOPQRSTUVWXYZ
abcdefghijklm
nopqrstuvwxyz
1234567890

COLOR

C5 M80 Y84 K0
C4 M47 Y15 K0
C89 M47 Y90 K10
C12 M11 Y89 K0

GRAPHIC

Let's keep in touch in case you get hungry
info@earlybird.com
+41 830 420 195
earlybird

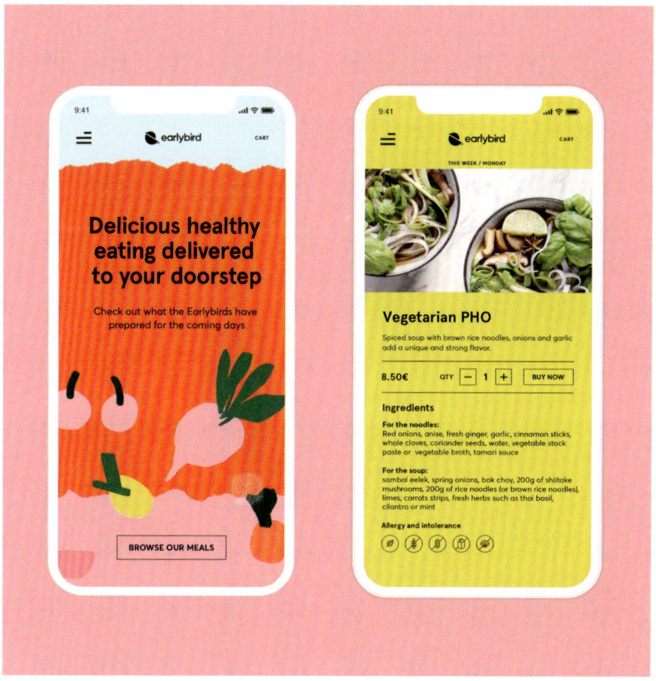
earlybird
CART
Delicious healthy eating delivered to your doorstep
Check out what the Earlybirds have prepared for the coming days
BROWSE OUR MEALS
earlybird
CART
Vegetarian PHO
Spiced soup with brown rice noodles, onions and garlic add a unique and strong flavor.
8.50€
QTY
BUY NOW
Ingredients
For the noodles:
Red onions, anise, fresh ginger, garlic, cinnamon sticks, whole cloves, coriander seeds, water, vegetable stock paste or vegetable broth, tamari sauce
For the soup:
sambal eelek, spring onions, bok choy, 200g of shiitake mushrooms, 200g of rice noodles (or brown rice noodles), limes, carrots strips, fresh herbs such as thai basil, cilantro or mint
Allergy and intolerance

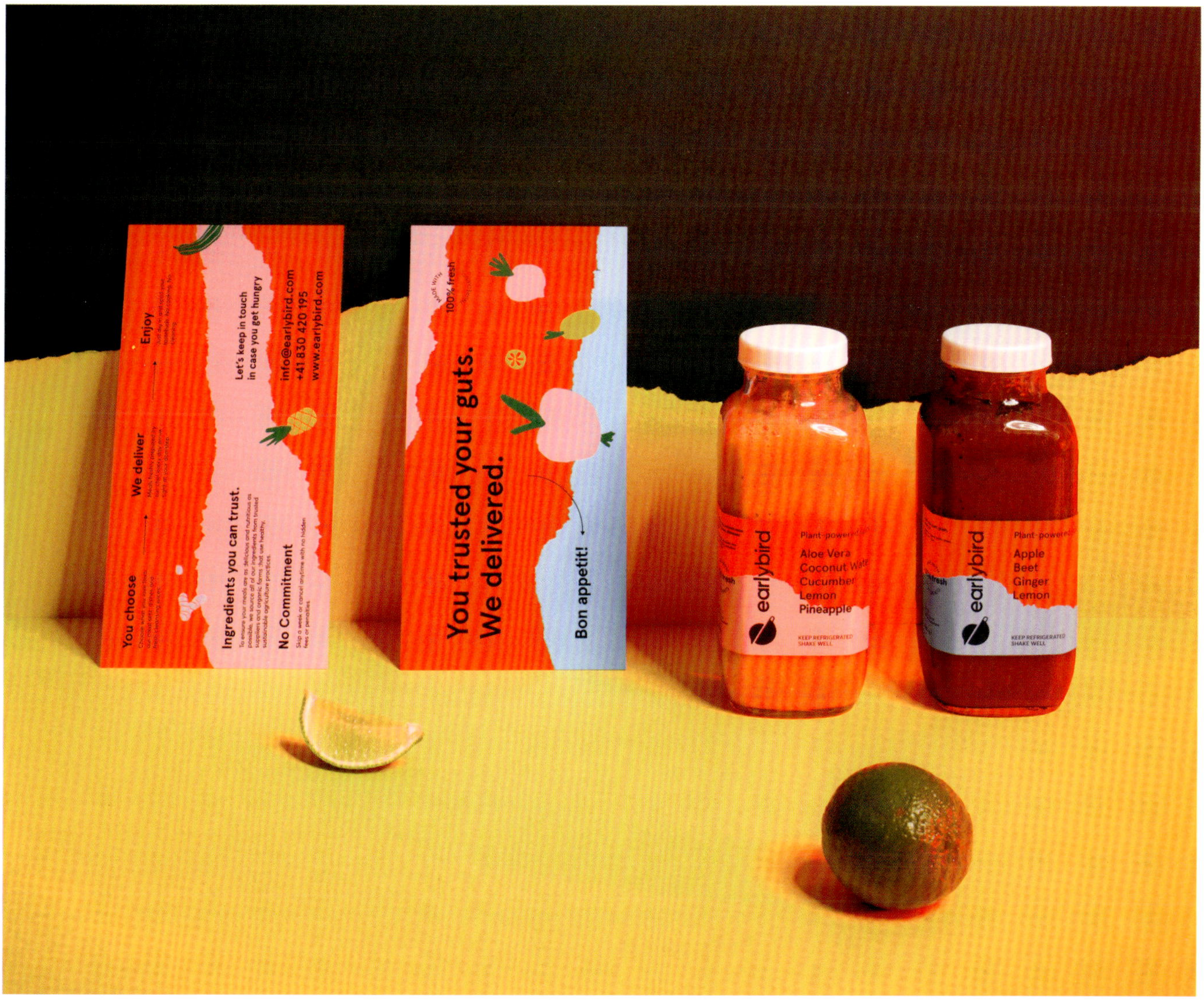
You choose
We deliver
Enjoy
Ingredients you can trust.
No Commitment
Let's keep in touch in case you get hungry
info@earlybird.com
+41 830 420 195
www.earlybird.com
100% fresh
You trusted your guts.
We delivered.
Bon appetit!
earlybird
Aloe Vera
Cucumber
Lemon
Pineapple
earlybird
Apple
Beet
Ginger
Lemon

COP 25th Global Climate Change Conference

Design Agency • **Shangning Wang Graphic Design**
Art Direction • **Shangning Wang**
Design • **Shangning Wang**

The United Nations Climate Change Conferences are yearly conferences. When Shangning reviewed the previous years' branding designs, he found them too common and normal. Hence, he decided to rebrand the conference and make this self-initiated project. The objective of this project was to create an attractive brand identity that reflects the connection between the weather and global climate change, raising awareness around this critical topic.

LOGO

COP25

FONT · Custom Font

ABCDEFGHIJ
KLMNOPQRST
UVWXYZ
1234567890

COLOR

C60 M0 Y3 K0
C0 M10 Y95 K0
C85 M50 Y0 K0
C0 M90 Y85 K0

GRAPHIC

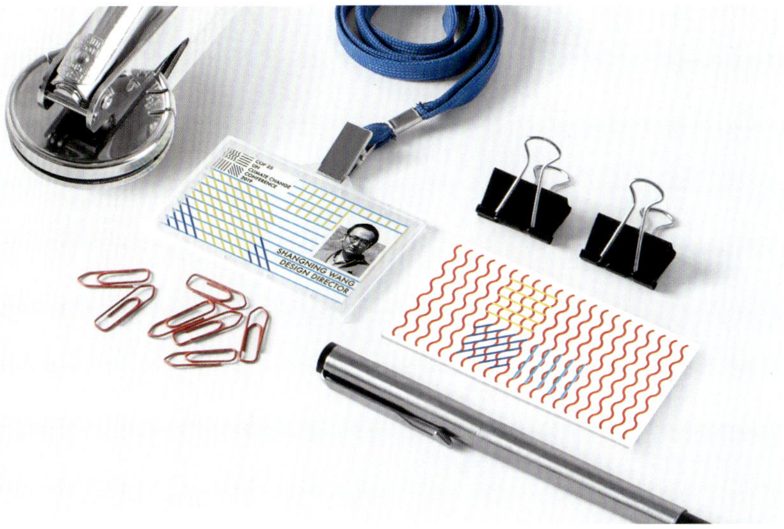
SHANGNING WANG
DESIGN DIRECTOR

COP 25
UN
CLIMATE CHANGE
CONFERENCE
2019
UNFCCC COP 25

COP25 UNFCCC 2019
DIESEL
533

Legend Fun

Art Direction • **Stella Shih**
Design • **Stella Shih**
Photography • **Eugene Lee**

This project was executed for a store located in the Shilin District of Taipei that specializes in board games. The conceptual theme of a table was used as the guiding principle in the overall store design. The store logo is composed of the letters of the store's name, Legend Fun, and morphs them into the four corners of a table. The business's promotional fliers can be folded along dotted lines to create small paper tables and this 3D concept was brought into the interior space of the shop as well, influencing the design of the front counter, door sign, menu, and even the paper bathroom sign.

LOGO

FONT · DIN Bold

ABCDEFGHIJKLM
NOPQRSTUVWXYZ
abcdefghijklm
nopqrstuvwxyz
1234567890

COLOR

C100 M100 Y0 K0

GRAPHIC

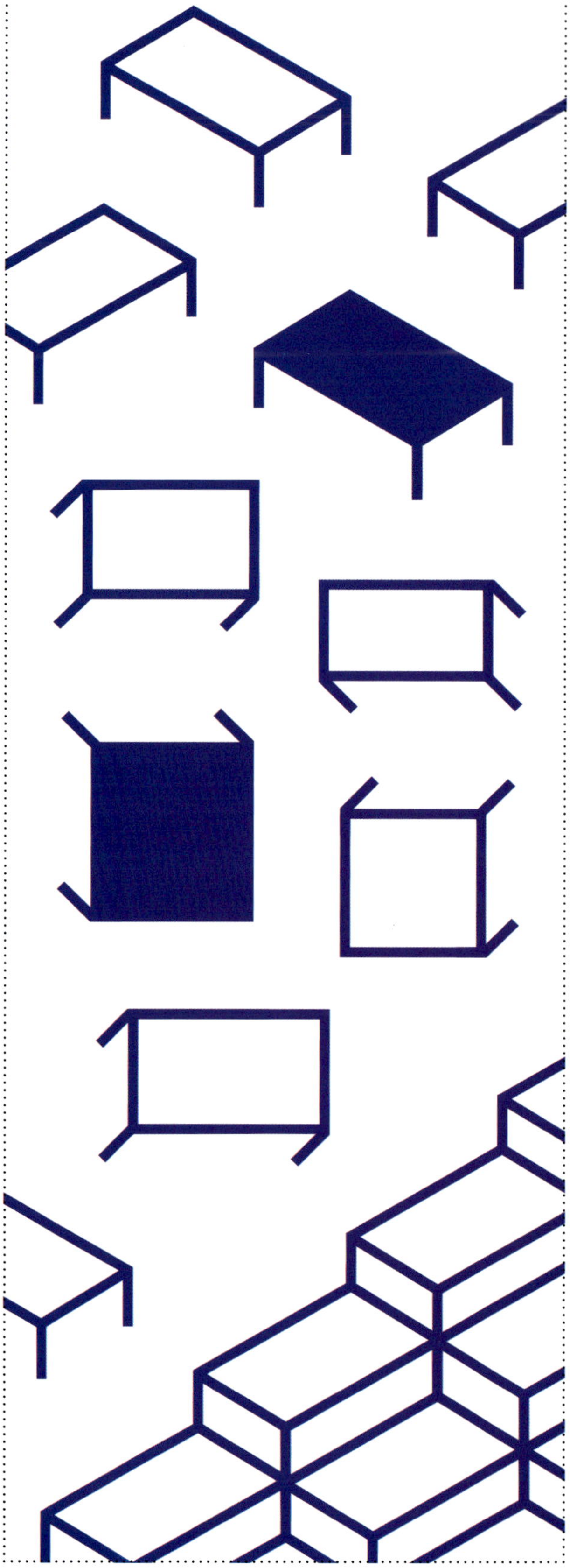

LEGEND FUN

LEGEND FUN

2016
GRAND
LEGEND FUN
PLAY
OPENING
Mon. 12:00 - 21

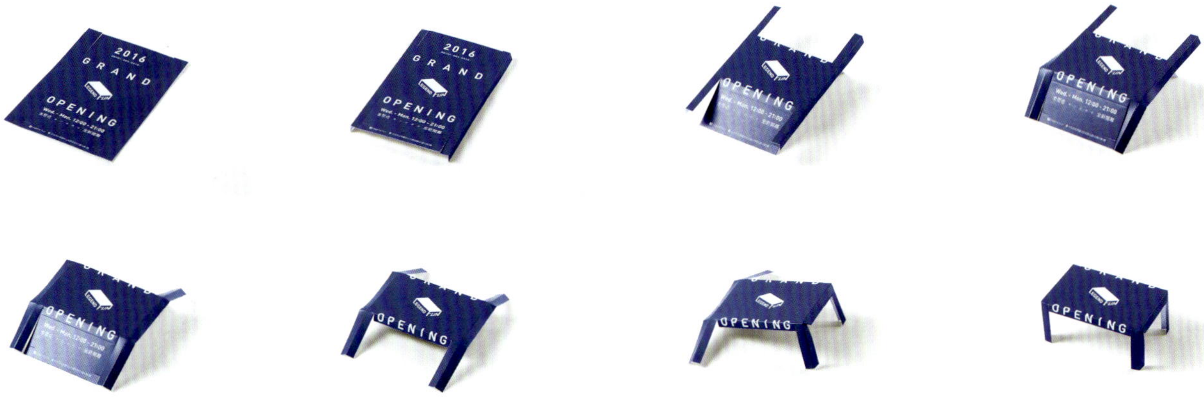

MENü
咖啡
美式咖啡 $75
拿鐵 $95
愛爾蘭咖啡 $110
貝禮詩拿鐵 $110
黑糖牛奶/拿鐵 $100
抹茶牛奶/拿鐵 $100
可可 $100
茶/果汁
錫蘭紅茶 $70
鮮奶茶 $80
水果茶 $100
鮮榨果汁 $90
HAVE A NICE PLAY!
季節飲
冬瓜檸檬 $80
薑母茶 $80
罐裝
原萃綠茶 $25
可樂 $20
水 $20
小東西
貝果 $45
貝果 $55
薯條 $120
雞柳條 $120
杏鮑菇 $120
綜合拼盤 $220

士林
樂聚坊
中山北路五段
505巷44弄
2

OPEN
HOUR
Wed. - Mon.
Hello,
welcome to
our
board game store
LEGEND
FUN

Funfunny

Design • Gilian Gomes

Funfunny is a children's clothing brand based in Porto Alegre, Brazil. The goal of Gilian Gomes was to design a brand identity which is cheerful and fluffy but at the same time elegant and sophisticated. The symbol proposed, a smiling face with an incorporated lower-case "f," is neutral, valuing diversity. Gilian designed one face that allows for numerous applications, emphasizing the diversity of gender present in the brand. For typography and visual construction, the shape of the circle was respected as a standard element. The rounded corners contribute to the logotype's soft and friendly appearance.

LOGO

Funfunny

FONT • NeutraText

ABCDEFGHIJKLM
NOPQRSTUVWXYZ
abcdefghijklm
nopqrstuvwxyz
1234567890

COLOR

C96 M80 Y0 K0

C0 M50 Y20 K0

GRAPHIC

Funfunny

Funfunny
it´s so
funfunny!

more fun
less phone

funfunny
Funfunny
it´s so
funfunny!
Funfunny
less phone
more fun

Funfunny
Funfunny
Funfunny
Funfunny
a funfunny
way to dress
Funfunny
Funfunny

Kaiju Company

Design Agency • **LIE DESIGN & ART DIRECTION**
Art Direction • **Driv Loo**
Design • **Driv Loo**
Client • **Kaiju Company**
Photography • **SmashPop**

Kaiju is a Thai-Japanese fusion restaurant in Kuala Lumpur. LIE helped to set the overall mood and tone of the restaurant, designing the brand identities, the menu and name card. During the design production, LIE worked closely with the interior designer to develop the visual identity by infusing the restaurant with Thai and Japanese style. Inspired by the name *kaiju*, which means "giant monsters," LIE used Godzilla and a Thai Dragon as the restaurant's emblems.

LOGO

ร้านอาหาร
kaiju
怪獣

FONT • Garamond Pro

ABCDEFGHIJKLM
NOPQRSTUVWXYZ
abcdefghijklm
nopqrstuvwxyz
1234567890

COLOR

C6 M80 Y0 K0

GRAPHIC

怪獣號
カイジュウ
Thai Style
Ryōri
kaiju
k

kaiju
Kaiju. Thai Style Ryōri.
Lot S4, APW Bangsar.
29 Jalan Riong,
59100 Kuala Lumpur.
+603 2788 3796
FB. IG. KaijuCompany
k

Opening Hours.
Thai Style
Ryōri
kaiju
#KaijuCompany

Identity of "Пили-швили"

Design Agency • **Dorogobogato Design Bureau**
Design • **Roman Novozhilov, Nikita Kanarev, Sasha Gordienko**
Illustration • **Sasha Gordienko**
Photography • **Oleg Truevtsev**

"Пили-швили" is a restaurant of Caucasian cuisine in Barnaul, Russia. Dorogobogato Design Bureau based the restaurant's identity on the art of Niko Pirosmani, the famous representative of primitivism who depicted the life and age-old traditions of real Georgians. The designers drew over a hundred Georgians at a feast, a common theme of Pirosmani's. They also developed a whimsical, strange font based on the logo. The main color in the design identity is brown. It is warm and traditional and combines perfectly with the natural materials that were used in the interior of the restaurant.

LOGO

ПИЛИ–ШВИЛИ
РЕСТОРАН КАВКАЗСКОЙ КУХНИ

FONT • Custom Font

ABCDEFGHI
JKLMNOPQR
STUVWXYZ
1234567890

COLOR

C55 M60 Y60 K80
C20 M45 Y20 K0
C18 M30 Y65 K0

GRAPHIC

МЕНЮ
ПИЛИ–ШВИЛИ
РЕСТОРАН КАВКАЗСКОЙ КУХНИ
ПИЛИ–ШВИЛИ
РЕСТОРАН КАВКАЗСКОЙ КУХНИ
вс-чт 12:00-24:00
пт-сб 12:00-02:00
Ленина 44-а
@pili_shvili
8 (3852)20-20-20

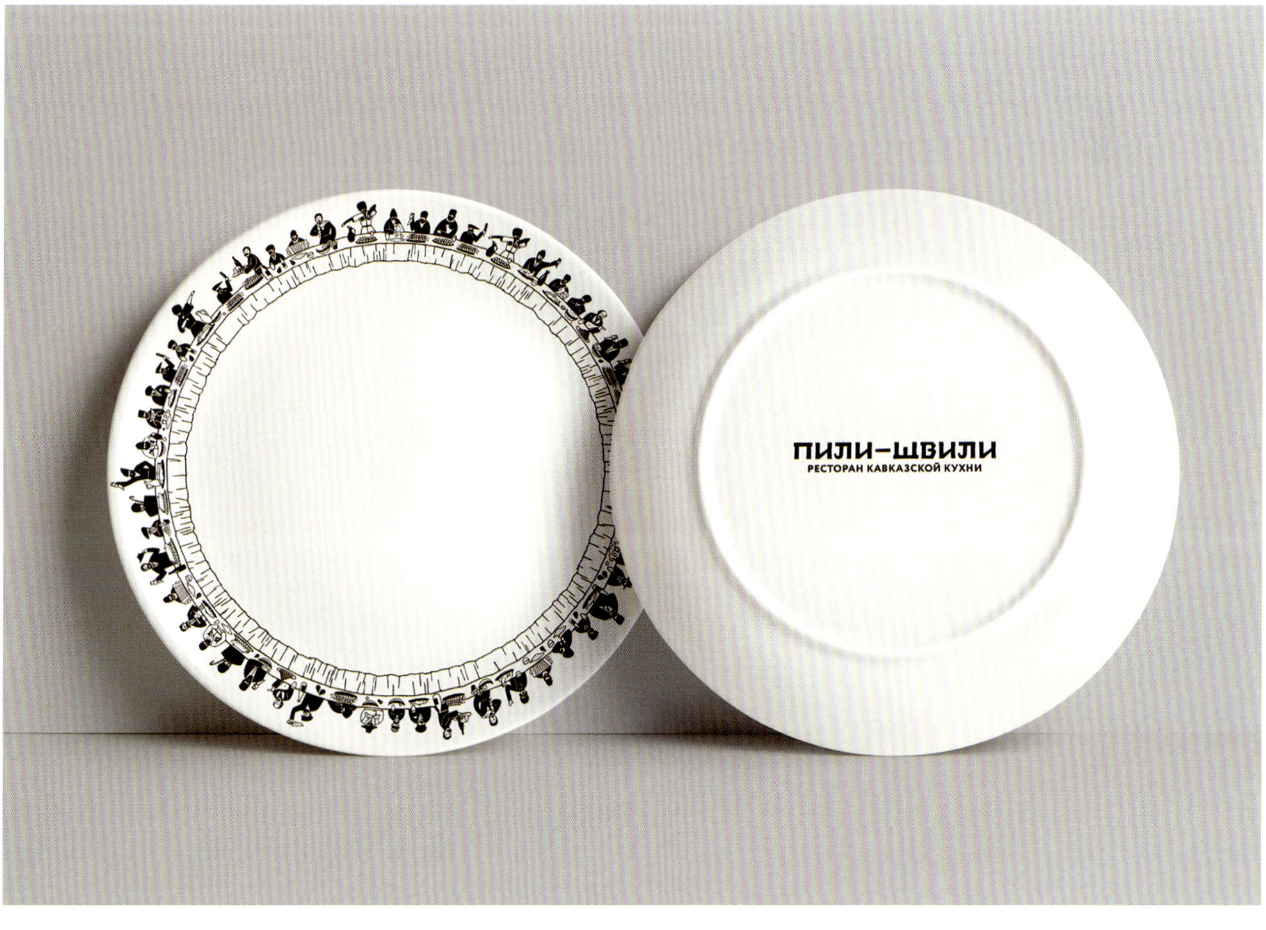
ПИЛИ–ШВИЛИ
РЕСТОРАН КАВКАЗСКОЙ КУХНИ

СТОЛ ЗАКАЗАН
МЕНЮ
ПИЛИ–ШВИЛИ

10
ПИЛИ–ШВИЛИ
ПИЛИ–ШВИЛИ
РЕСТОРАН КАВКАЗСКОЙ КУХНИ

ПИЛИ-ШВИЛИ
РЕСТОРАН КАВКАЗСКОЙ КУХНИ

TAIKIN

Art Direction • **Oscar Bastidas**
Design • **Oscar Bastidas**
Illustration • **Oscar Bastidas**
Photography • **Oscar Bastidas**

Taikin is a deluxe Japanese restaurant located in Miami, Florida. Oscar Bastidas's challenge was to find the most interesting stories of Japanese mythology that had not been used for commercial purposes, and then to incorporate them into the graphic elements for the restaurant's identity and interior design. *Taikin*, which means "fortune," is linked to the *tanuki*, a Japanese raccoon dog. This character is the main part of the restaurant's graphic story, a branding design full of illustrations and details.

LOGO

FONT • Klinic Slab

ABCDEFGHIJKLM
NOPQRSTUVWXYZ
abcdefghijklm
nopqrstuvwxyz
1234567890

COLOR

C0 M89 Y95 K0
C21 M17 Y33 K0
C0 M0 Y0 K100

GRAPHIC

TAIKIN

TAIKIN
TAIKIN

TAIKIN

SALAD
COCONUT SOUP | Chicken, coconut milk

TAIKIN
TAIKINASIAN
TAIKIN

"KITSUNE" (Fox) or the "NEKOMATA" (Cat) who also has magic powers.
たぬき
酒
Tanukis can be naughty! They often adopt human shapes to get into bars and transform leaves into coins to buy sake.

Avacorp

Design Agency • **Menta Picante**
Design • **Alex Román, Gaby Salazar**

Avacorp is a real estate appraisal company in Guadalajara with over twenty years in the market. They were looking to project a new and fresh image that communicated their way of working. Therefore, Menta Picante created a visual system composed of three real estate maps: commercial, residential and industrial. The logotype is a simple typeface, creating a contrasting duality with the fun illustrations.

LOGO

AVACORP®

FONT · Alpinist

ABCDEFGHIJKLM
NOPQRSTUVWXYZ
abcdefghijklm
nopqrstuvwxyz
1234567890

COLOR

C0 M80 Y69 K0

GRAPHIC

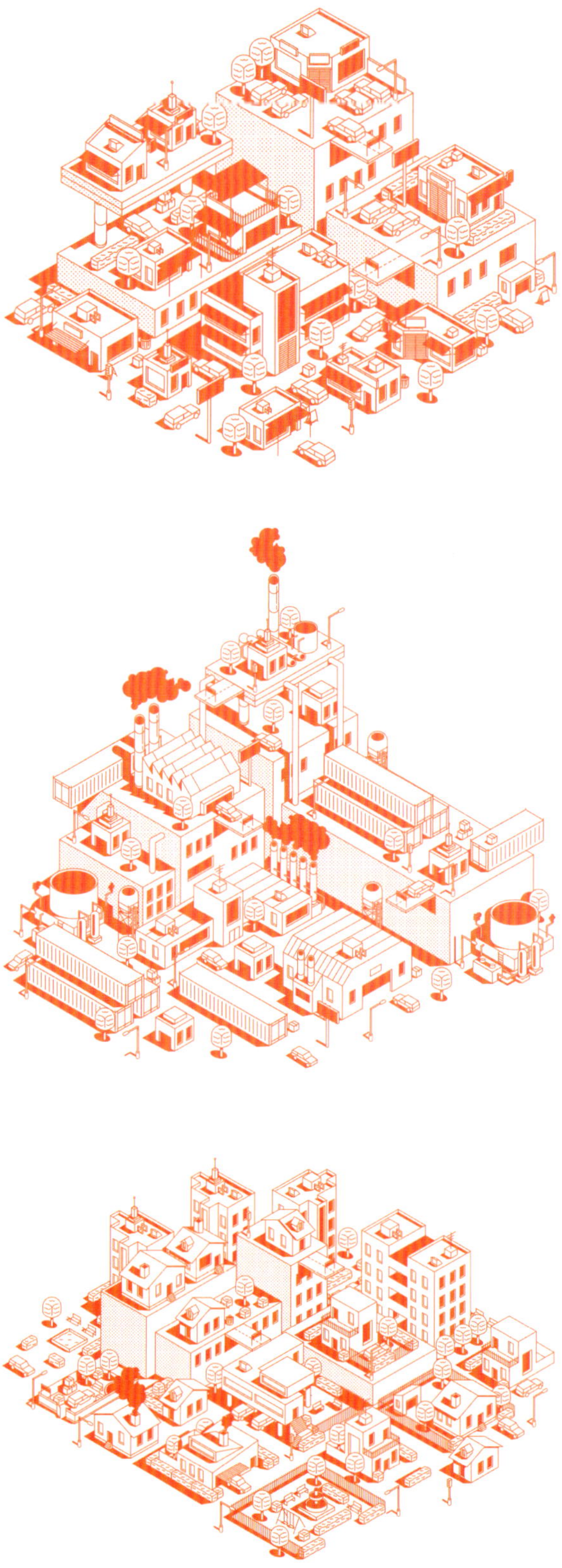

AVACORP
Ostia 2585, Col. Providencia
Guadalajara - Jalisco.
Tel. — 01 33 3641 0402
— 01 33 3640 3229
avacorp.com.mx

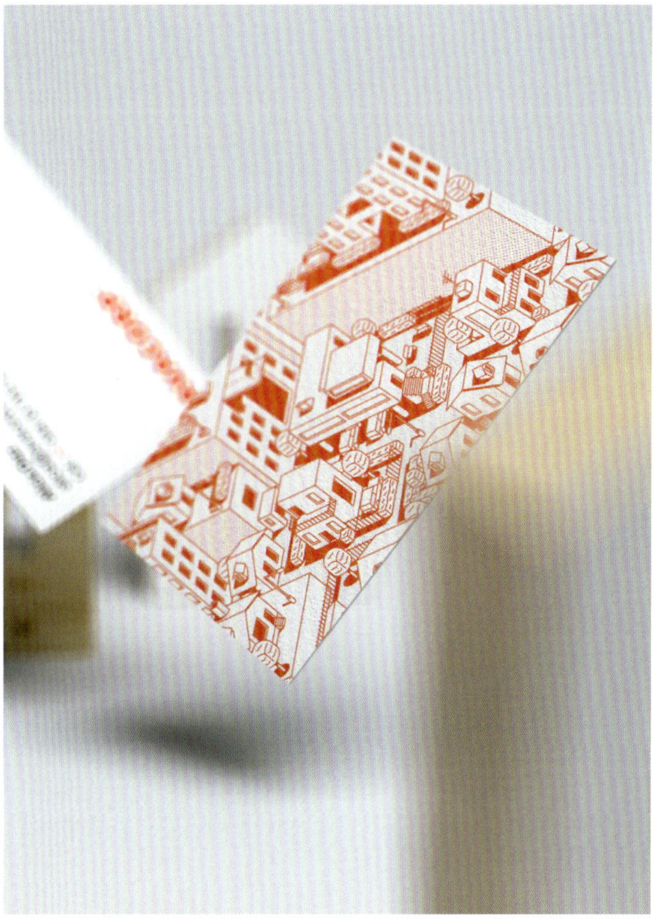

Trabajamos para proteger tu inversión.
avacorp.com.mx
AVACORP
AVACORP
AVACORP
AVACORP
TENDENCIAS DEL MERCADO

The Meat Preachers

Design Agency • **makebardo**

The Meat Preachers is a casual restaurant known for its grilled meats. Makebardo's main goal was to create an identity that appeals to everyone through a friendly, authentic and fresh design approach. The lines behind the brand characters are reminiscent of the musical staff, suggesting the harmony of flavors, and at the same time symbolize the grill and the cooking technique that make this restaurant unique. The burnt orange color, suggesting fire, pushes these associations further. Makebardo chose serif typeface for its lavish flair and its sense of tradition, quality, and balance.

LOGO

The Meat Preachers

FONT • Saol Text - Bold

ABCDEFGHIJKLM
NOPQRSTUVWXYZ
abcdefghijklm
nopqrstuvwxyz
1234567890

COLOR

C0 M79 Y100 K0

GRAPHIC

themeatpreachers.com

We source
all our meat
from a select
number of
South Island
producers.
@themeatpreachers.com

The Meat
Preachers
Open every day from:
11am to 9pm
Queenstown Central B-09
Grant Rd, Frankton
New Zealand
#themeatpreachers
+64 03 409 0265
hi@themeatpreachers.com
We source all our
meat from a select
number of South
Island producers.

Ale Lipa

Design Agency • **Fajne Chlopaki**
Art Direction • **Fajne Chlopaki**
Illustration • **Łukasz Zbieranowski**
Photography • **Piter Trojanowski**

Ale Lipa is a bistro in Lodz, Poland that stands in a neighborhood where there was a linden forest a hundred years ago. The restaurant's visual identification came from the land itself; Fajne Chlopaki's goal was to direct it to the right track. Inspired by the forest, nature, and wood, Fajne Chlopaki created a handmade identity for Ale Lipa that reflects the bistro's emphasis on good quality.

LOGO

ALE LIPA
NA POLESIU

FONT · Qiber

ABCDEFGHIJKLM
NOPQRSTUVWXYZ
abcdefghijklm
nopqrstuvwxyz
1234567890

COLOR

C0 M0 Y0 K100

GRAPHIC

ALE LIPA
NA POLESIU
INFORMACJA DLA ALERGIKÓW: NIE MA LIPY

ALE LIPA
NA POLESIU
ALE LIPA
NA POLESIU

Ricefields

Creative Direction • **Tony Ibbotson**
Design • **Emma Lucia Newnes**

Sourcing three different varieties of organic rice from the lush fields of China, Japan, and the Himalayas, Ricefields brings quality authentic ingredients to the table. Taking inspiration from the lines and form of rice paddies all over the world, Emma designed the logo with colors taken from the different types of harvested rice, signifying the origin of rice and telling a story about the staple ingredient. The goal of the visual identity was to bring romance to dining at Ricefields, to educate diners about where the food comes from, and to celebrate the art of rice harvesting from different parts of the world.

LOGO

Ricefields

FONT · Custom Font

abcdefghij
klmnopqr
stuvwxyz
1234567890

COLOR

C94 M45 Y65 K37
C18 M100 Y74 K8
C0 M23 Y11 K0

GRAPHIC

Ricefields
Premium Bowls
ph. 02 9123 4567
store 135 pitt st sydney

Bowls
Sides
Drinks
Menu

Ricefields

ASTE WITH
A STORY

FROM
FIELD
TO TABL
FROM
FIELD
TO TABLE

Ricefields
Ricefields
Ricefields

National Marine Center

Design • **Pauline Pourcelot**

National Marine Center is a branding project about a fictional marine reserve built as a glass tube that plunges underwater. Inspired by the lack of gravity underwater, Pauline Pourcelot designed the logo with the thought that if fishes were to write words, they would let the letters float. The design of the visual identity of the aquarium explores the fish dynamics and the variety of algae thanks to watercolor illustrations.

LOGO

National
Marine
Center

FONT · Minimal Mono

ABCDEFGHIJKLM
NOPQRSTUVWXYZ
abcdefghijklm
nopqrstuvwxyz
1234567890

COLOR

C44 M7 Y27 K0
C67 M15 Y19 K0
C100 M85 Y40 K39
C6 M10 Y33 K0

GRAPHIC

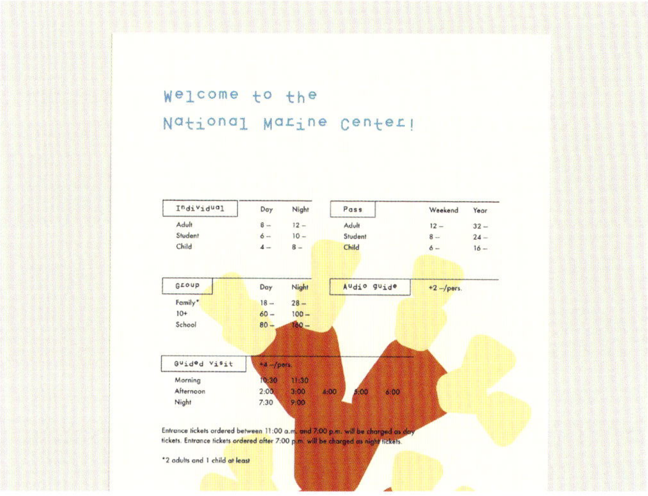
Welcome to the
National Marine Center!
Individual Day Night
Adult 8 – 12 –
Student 6 – 10 –
Child 4 – 8 –
Pass Weekend Year
Adult 12 – 32 –
Student 8 – 24 –
Child 6 – 16 –
Group Day Night
Family* 18 – 28 –
10+ 60 – 100 –
School 80 – 160 –
Audio guide +2 –/pers.
Guided visit +4 –/pers.
Morning 10:30 11:30
Afternoon 2:00 3:00 4:00 5:00 6:00
Night 7:30 9:00
Entrance tickets ordered between 11:00 a.m. and 7:00 p.m. will be charged as day tickets. Entrance tickets ordered after 7:00 p.m. will be charged as night tickets.
*2 adults and 1 child at least

Staff
National Marine Center

National Marine Center

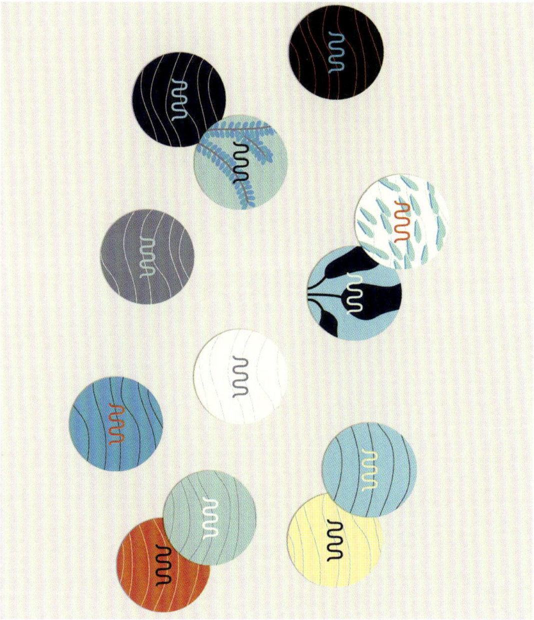

Easy, Tiger

Design Agency • **Serious Studio**

Easy, Tiger is a quick-service restaurant in Manila that serves authentic Thai food. To create the concept, Serious Studio took pieces of inspiration from Thailand's vibrant culture: traditional batik patterns, street vendor kitsch, and the fighting art style of Muay Thai. Given the restaurant's food-hall format, they made sure to create a brand that was easy to understand, yet exciting enough to pack a punch.

LOGO

FONT • NiveauSerif

ABCDEFGHIJKLM
NOPQRSTUVWXYZ
abcdefghijklm
nopqrstuvwxyz
1234567890

COLOR

C0 M57 Y100 K0

C0 M10 Y54 K0

C0 M0 Y0 K100

C0 M91 Y92 K60

GRAPHIC

EASY,
TIGER
THAI FOOD
WITH A KICK
ROUNDS
MEAL SETS
HIGH KICK!
WITH A PUNCH!
GRILLED BACON BELLY
CHICKEN PANDAN
RED CURRY BEEF
CHIANGMAI SAUSAGE
SATE CHICKEN
GREEN CURRY CHICKEN
GRILLED CHICKEN 999
SATE BACON BELLY
TOFU & VEGETABLE CURRY 999
TIGER
CHOK!
BAM
SOMTAM
CATFISH MANGO SALAD

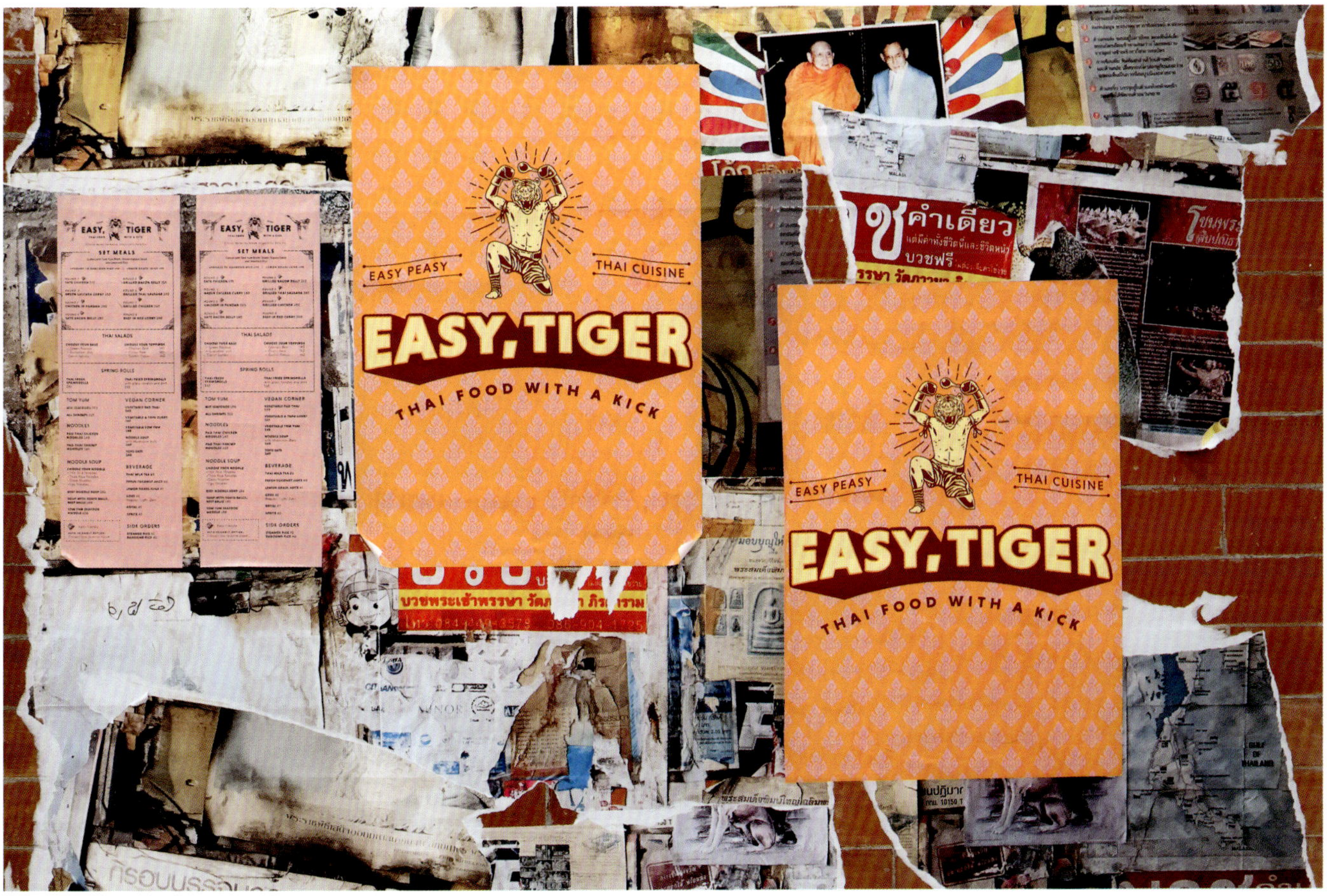
EASY PEASY
THAI CUISINE
EASY, TIGER
THAI FOOD WITH A KICK
EASY PEASY
THAI CUISINE
EASY, TIGER
THAI FOOD WITH A KICK

Kombinat Restaurant

Design Agency • **Flat12**
Art Direction • **Yana Klochikhina**
Design • **Anton Skalkin**
Client • **BB Group Holding Company**

Kombinat is a casual seafood and fish restaurant. The identity reflects the architectural manifestation of the place, as a contemporary adaptation of a Soviet industrial site. The minimalistic geometric forms, simple lines, and restrained color palette echo the style of Soviet-era city signs.

LOGO

FISH AND SEAFOOD
KOMBINAT

FONT • Merel

A B C D E F G H I J K L M
N O P Q R S T U V W X Y Z
a b c d e f g h i j k l m
n o p q r s t u v w x y z

COLOR

C50 M35 Y0 K80
C0 M10 Y19 K5
C0 M33 Y40 K48
C0 M2 Y3 K2

GRAPHIC

РЫБА И НЕ ТОЛЬКО
КОМБИНАТ
ИМЯ СОТРУДНИКА
КОМБИНАТ
ИМЯ СОТРУДНИКА

РЫБА И НЕ ТОЛЬКО
КОМБИНАТ

Le Crois

Design Agency • **Hue Studio**
Creative Direction • **Vian Risanto**
Design • **Vian Risanto, Adela Saputra**
Illustration • **Vian Risanto**
Photography • **Jave Hoonl**

Le Crois is a bakery and cafe located at The Glen Shopping Centre in Victoria, Australia. Le Crois is a mix of Asian and French signature tastes. The logo was inspired by the shape of a croissant, the iconic French pastry, yet conceptualized to reflect a modern twist in the branding. It can be seen in the design on the stackable coffee cups, which showcase this beautiful twisting pattern. The contrast color is a reflection of the brand's values, imparting a modern, fun and fresh nuance.

LOGO

Le Crois

FONT • Geomanist

ABCDEFGHIJKLM
NOPQRSTUVWXYZ
abcdefghijklm
nopqrstuvwxyz
1234567890

COLOR

C3 M37 Y33 K0

C38 M23 Y56 K7

GRAPHIC

Le Crois
Le Crois

Le Crois

Le Crois
Le Crois
Le Crois
Le Crois

Enso

Design Agency • **Basic Studio**
Design • **Erik Villarreal García, Ana Lucía González Sánchez**
Photography • **Karina Zertuche**

ENSO is a brand that encourages spiritual wellness and emotional stability through art therapies. Basic Studio designed a brand system based on the graphic of the Japanese symbol " 円相 "—the moment when the mind is free to let the body create. The brand is composed of a series of illustrations that symbolize enlightenment, self-knowledge, and tranquility through a minimal Japanese aesthetic.

LOGO

FONT • Contax Sans

ABCDEFGHIJKLM
NOPQRSTUVWXYZ
abcdefghijklm
nopqrstuvwxyz
1234567890

COLOR

C0 M64 Y46 K0
C41 M0 Y24 K0
C33 M16 Y11 K0
C15 M13 Y15 K0

GRAPHIC

ENSO
Conocimiento
Balance
Crecimiento
ENSO
Taller Grupal

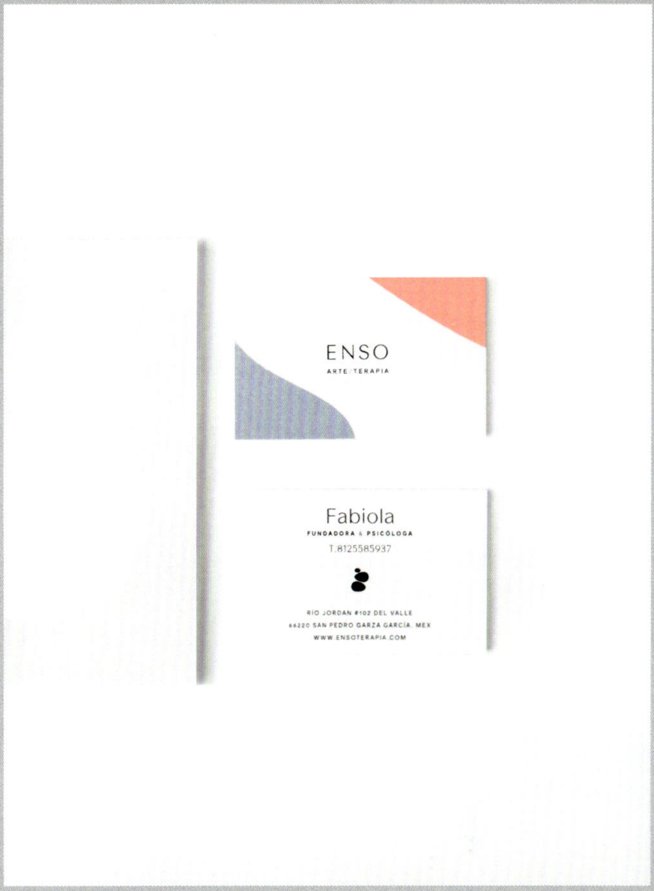
ENSO
ARTE:TERAPIA
Fabiola
FUNDADORA & PSICÓLOGA
T.8125585937
RIO JORDAN #102 DEL VALLE
66220 SAN PEDRO GARZA GARCÍA, MEX
WWW.ENSOTERAPIA.COM

Grupal

OCHAYA MATCHA

Design Agency • **Kinoto Studio**
Design • **Monica Reyes**

Kinoto Studio was asked to design a brand for a matcha company called Ochaya from Lima, Peru. The logo had to represent the freshness, sophistication, and history of a product that originally comes from Japan. Kinoto Studio's inspiration came from the Japanese culture of tea, and they based the project on elements from traditional teahouses and the ceremony of matcha tea.
For the design of the packaging, they had to think of a graphics system that could work for all of the product varieties. Kinoto Studio wanted to keep some of the simplicity of Japanese graphic design, illustration, and typography.

LOGO

お茶屋
ÔCHAYA
TEA HOUSE

FONT • Courier

ABCDEFGHIJKLM
NOPQRSTUVWXYZ
abcdefghijklm
nopqrstuvwxyz
1234567890

COLOR

C5 M50 Y36 K0
C42 M65 Y11 K0
C59 M7 Y38 K0
C13 M65 Y87 K0

GRAPHIC

ÔCHAYA
MATCHA
ÔCHAYA
GENMAICHA
ÔCHAYA
HOJICHA

ÔCHAYA
HOJICHA
TEA HOUSE
お茶屋
132 GR.
MADE IN LIMA, PERU
ÔCHAYA
SENCHA
TEA HOUSE
お茶屋
132 GR.
MADE IN LIMA, PERU
ÔCHAYA
MATCHA
TEA HOUSE
お茶屋
132 GR.
MADE IN LIMA, PERU
ÔCHAYA
GENMAICHA
TEA HOUSE
お茶屋
132 GR.
MADE IN LIMA, PERU

MATCHA
Es el té verde que se elabora sin triturar las hojas y el más consumido en Japón. Es una mezcla armoniosa de dulzura, amargura, astringencia y fragancia. La bebida perfecta para revitalizar la mente y refrescar el espíritu.
RICO EN ANTIOXIDANTES
ACELERA EL METABOLISMO
CAFEÍNA NATURAL
DULZURA IDEAL PARA POSTRES
ORIGEN: Shizuoka, Japón.
NIVEL DE CAFEÍNA: Medio
PREPARACIÓN
Pon 1 gr de té en una taza
1 gr.
Luego 70 ml de agua caliente
Bate con un chasen o con un batidor ¡Disfruta!
ÔCHAYA
USDA ORGANIC
Envasado en Lima, Perú.
Producto 100% Natural
5 901234 123457
SENCHA
HOJICHA

TARGI RZECZY ŁADNYCH

Design Agency • **Walk with David**
Design • **Aleksandra Lampart**

Targi Rzeczy Ładnych ("Fair of Pretty Things") is the biggest design fair in Warsaw. The purpose of the event is to promote and popularize quality designs available to the general public. Walk with David's goal was to design a modern but also friendly and memorable visual identification. The idea behind the new system—"open the box, look in the middle"—led to the minimalist and mobile logo which changes its form depending on the context.

LOGO

Targi
Rzeczy
Ładnych

FONT · Futura

ABCDEFGHIJKLM
NOPQRSTUVWXYZ
abcdefghijklm
nopqrstuvwxyz
1234567890

COLOR

C32 M4 Y6 K0

C0 M30 Y6 K0

GRAPHIC

Zegar
40 zł

Targi
Rzeczy
ładnych
Targi
Rzeczy
ładnych
Targi
Rzeczy
ładnych
Targi
Rzeczy
ładnych

Doniczka
59 zł
Lampa
119 zł
Zegar
40 zł

Targi
Rzeczy
ładnych
ładny
bilet
Targi
Rzeczy
ładnych

BONA Restaurant

Design Agency • **Hmmm Creative Studio**
Art Direction • **Helene Vetik**
Creative Direction • **Karl Saluveer**
Design • **Andreas Roosson**
Client • **BONA Restaurant**
Illustration • **Andreas Roosson**

BONA used to be the "it" place in town, the best French restaurant in Estonia. But the white-linen style slowed down service and seemed outdated so a decision was made to refresh and rebrand the identity from the kitchen all the way to the name. With the combination of French and inspiration from Wes Anderson movies, Hmmm Creative Studio created a visual identity to help the restaurant back to its glory.

LOGO

BO
NA

FONT · BurfordBase

ABCDEFGHIJKLM
NOPQRSTUVWXYZ
ABCDEFGHIJKLM
NOPQRSTUVWXYZ
1234567890

COLOR

C0 M65 Y50 K0
C0 M14 Y20 K0
C0 M12 Y73 K0
C20 M2 Y2 K0

GRAPHIC

Bona is a resto and bar that's both cozy yet stylish, classic, but modern, exciting, yet familiar. Famous for it's wide variety of unique gin-cocktails, beers and wines for all the tastes and a food menu thats hard to forget. See for yourself.
LEIB
Bread
ÕLU & SIIDER
VEINID
BO
NA
GINI-KOKTEILID
-20%
ERVEERITUD
y, this table is booked

BO
NA
CHÂTEAU
GRENOUIL

Minister Brewery

Design Agency • **Ostecx Créative**
Art Direction • **Sébastien Ploszaj**
Client • **Minister Brewery**
Illustration • **Kinga Offert**

Is it still possible to stand out on a crowded, craft beer shelf? Together with the illustrator Kinga Offert, Ostecx Créative created the visual identity of Minister Brewery by focusing on the client's approach to the brand image and breaking down beer clichés. Richly illustrated packaging is an important part of the brand's world—in a surprising and humorous way, it tells the story of individual styles of beer. The young spirit and the urban and artistic positioning of the brewery packaging are the results of discussions with the brand owners.

LOGO

BROWAR
MINISTER

FONT • Custom Font

BROWAR
MINISTER

COLOR

C63 M0 Y55 K0
C16 M6 Y82 K0
C0 M44 Y13 K0
C65 M2 Y15 K0

GRAPHIC

Paradajz
paradajz
LOVE
TROPICAL APA

MEGA POP
PILS
Milky day
MILK SHAKE IPA
Ein Minister
HOPPY BERLI NER WEISSE
Ein Minister
MALINA
RASPBERRY BERLI NER WEISSE
paradajz
TROPICAL APA
Magic Spoon

Many Mornings

Design Agency • **Fajne Chlopaki**
Art Direction • **Fajne Chlopaki**
Illustration • **Łukasz Zbieranowski**
Photography • **Kasia Szewczyk, Maciek Butkowski**

Many Mornings is a sock brand based in Aleksandrów Łódzki, the sock capital of Poland. Fajne Chlopaki wanted to create an everyday atmosphere to show that socks are everywhere, and to suggest that these colorful socks will make your morning, as well as the rest of your day.

GRAPHIC

LOGO

MANY MORNINGS

FONT · DINPro

ABCDEFGHIJKLM
NOPQRSTUVWXYZ
abcdefghijklm
nopqrstuvwxyz
1234567890

COLOR

C85 M65 Y0 K0
C70 M10 Y20 K0
C0 M60 Y60 K0
C0 M10 Y100 K0

MANY MORNINGS

MANY MORNINGS
made in Poland
size: 43-46

Sprudelhof

Design • **Yuan Wang**

Sprudelhof, with a century of history in Hessen, Germany, is a courtyard with a hot spring. The inspiration for the typography design came from the arched corridor, whose wave-shaped exterior is closely connected to the theme of water. The graphics depict a group of people enjoying nature and the hot spring. The flush on everybody's cheeks is the key visual element, and also appears in the logo, signage, and other materials.

LOGO

SPRUDEL
HOF

FONT • Custom Font

A B C D E F G H I J
K L M N O P Q R S T
U V W X Y Z Ä Ö Ü ß

a b c d e f g h i j k l m n
o p q r s t u v w x y z ä ö ü ß
0 1 2 3 4 5 6 7 8 9

COLOR

C96 M82 Y0 K0

C63 M21 Y59 K0

GRAPHIC

SPRUDEL
HOF
Ludwigstraße 20.61231 Bad Nauheim

SPRUDEL
HOF
+ 49 6032 3495588
Ludwigstraße 20
61231 Bad Nauheim

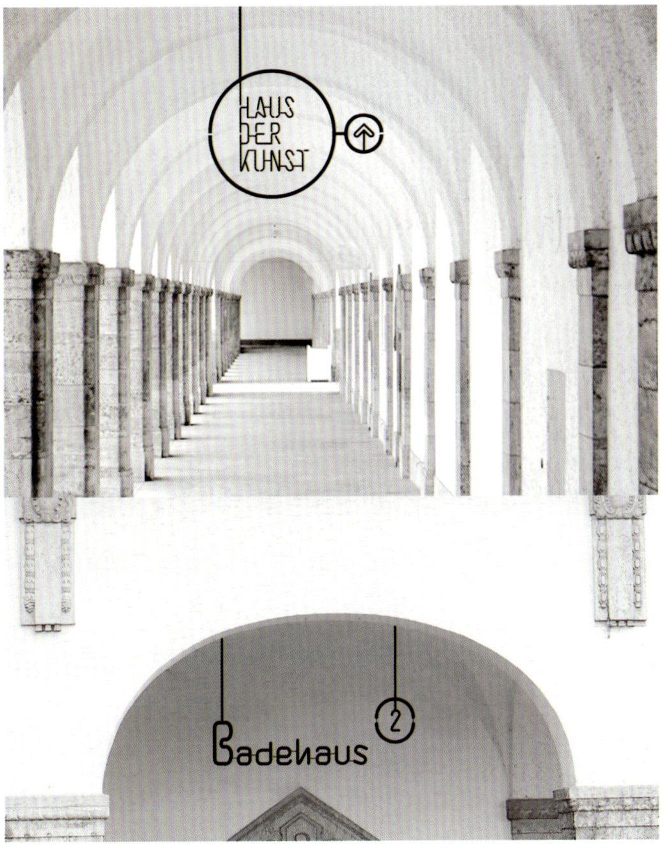
HAUS
DER
KUNST
Badehaus
2

HAUS
DER
KUNST

Bulls™ Garage & Garden Bar

Design Agency • **H3l Branding Agency**

The brand development of Bulls™ Garage & Garden Bar was addressed by the recognizable language of American dollar bills from different eras. The detailed work and the superposition of colors and plots illustrate the reference language. References of Asian lithographs were taken to configure the detail and proportions in the illustrations. For the menu, H3l Branding Agency also applied textures of leather, metals and rustic paper to show a binding experience evoking motorcycles, beer and night.

GRAPHIC

LOGO

BULLS
GARDEN BAR

FONT • TRY Vesterbro

ABCDEFGHIJKLM
NOPQRSTUVWXYZ
abcdefghijklm
nopqrstuvwxyz
1234567890

COLOR

C0 M82 Y94 K0

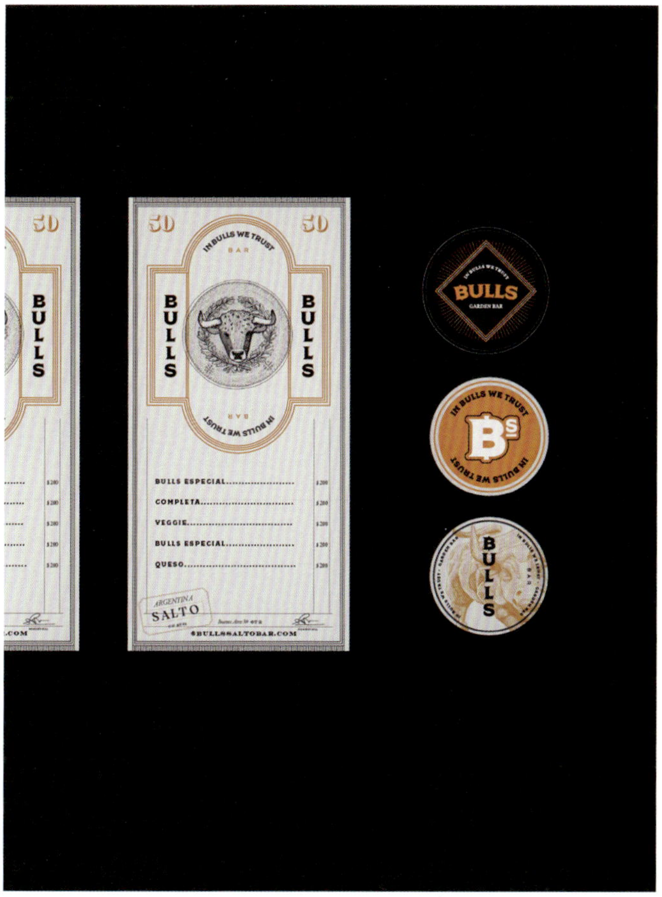
50
IN BULLS WE TRUST
BAR
BULLS
BULLS ESPECIAL
COMPLETA
VEGGIE
QUESO
SALTO
BULLS
GARDEN BAR

IN BULLS WE TRUST
BULLS

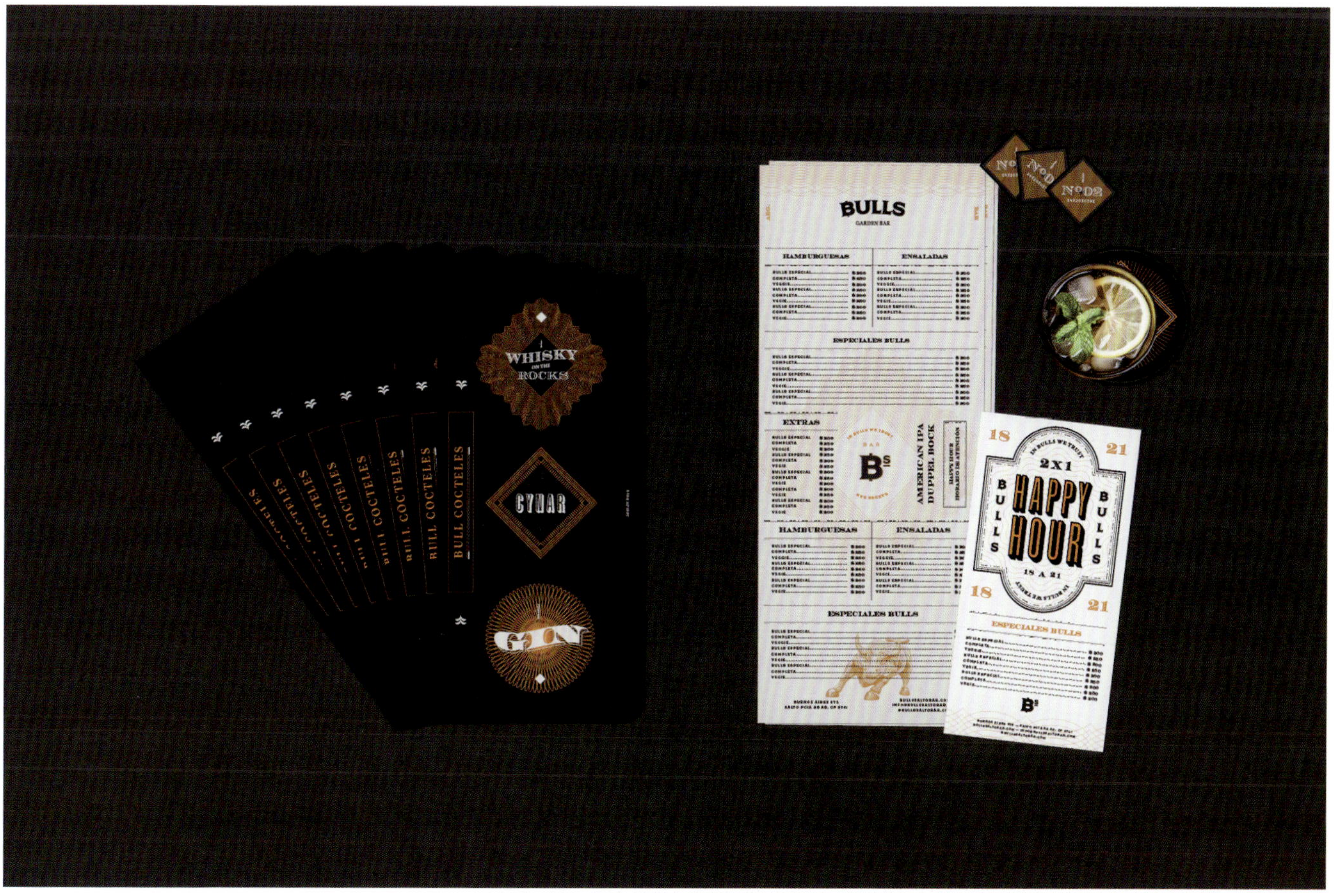
WHISKY
ON THE
ROCKS
CYNAR
GIN
BULL COCTELES
BULLS
GARDEN BAR
HAMBURGUESAS
ENSALADAS
ESPECIALES BULLS
EXTRAS
AMERICAN IPA
DUPPEL BOCK
18
21
2X1
HAPPY
HOUR
18 A 21
ESPECIALES BULLS

VERMOUTH
Nº02
IN BULLS WE TRUST
BAR
BULLS
BAR
IN BULLS WE TRUST
GIN

A
WHISKY ON THE ROCKS
1/2
GIN TONIC
GARAGE AND BEER
PINTA

IN BULLS WE TRUST
2x1
BULLS
HAPPY HOUR
BULLS
18 A 21
IN BULLS WE TRUST

GARAGE AND BEER
GARDEN BAR
Buenos Aires № 672
ARGENTINA
SALTO
WWW.BULLSSALTOBAR.COM

WARFIELD
MINER'S CANARY
IPA
IPA
LUCKY 7
IPA
RED IRISH

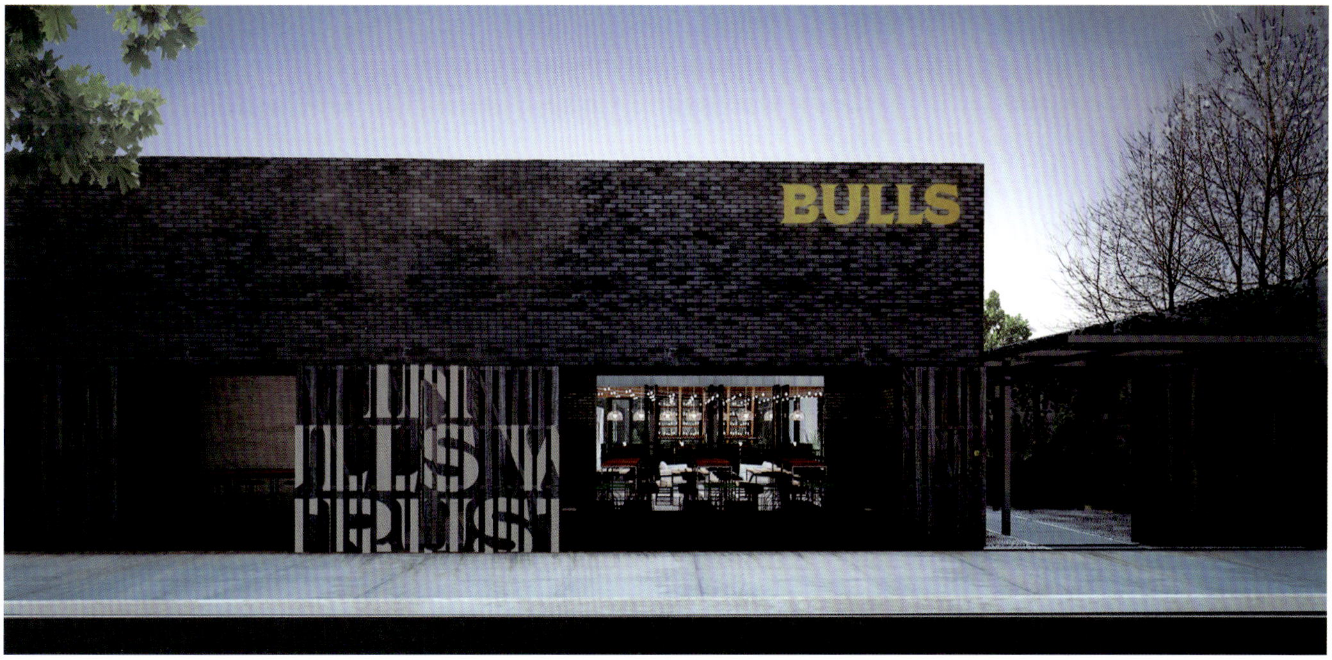
BULLS

LA TEQUILA

Design Agency • **MONOTYPO Studio**
Design • **Daniel Barba**
Client • **La Tequila Mexican Cuisine**
Photography • **Diana Cristina Espinoza**

La Tequila Mexican Cuisine is a proud exponent of Mexican cuisine. They follow the traditional recipes of the Mexican kitchen and improve them with contemporary intentions. With this project, they sought to graphically represent the best of Mexico, a nation that was built by a union between the past and the present, a rich cultural heritage from their pre-Hispanic roots. That same influence can be found in graphic arts, culture, language, clothing, and of course the food. MONOTYPO Studio looked to give a union in their restaurant through the use of old engravings, typography and visual elements with the purpose of providing the client with a gastronomic experience through Mexico.

LOGO

LATEQUILA
COCINA Ð MÉXICO

FONT · Custom Font

LATEQUILA
COCINA Ð MÉXICO

COLOR

C44 M61 Y66 K1

GRAPHIC

LATEQUILA

LATEQUILA
LATEQUILA
Av. México № 2830

Balloon & Whisk

Design Agency • **Thinking*Room**
Art Direction • **Eric Widjaja**
Design • **Ira Carella**

A cake shop in northern Jakarta, Balloon & Whisk sells various cookies, cakes, wine, and tea. These things, often, are not bought by people for themselves but as gifts for those they care about—a simple yet powerful display of endearment that reminds the receivers that they're on someone's mind. Balloon & Whisk's mission was to facilitate such sweet acts of gifting. The branding revolves around the themes of "light" and "air," characteristics shared by balloons and whisks—the balloon contains air, whereas whisks are a cooking utensil used to incorporate air into a mixture. The "light" theme is prominent as well in the illustrated characters, each representing different flavors and delicacies.

LOGO

FONT · Custom Font

COLOR

C56 M62 Y60 K5
C13 M19 Y7 K0
C25 M7 Y20 K0
C16 M31 Y25 K0

GRAPHIC

BALLOON
&WHISK

BALLOON
&WHISK
HUGO
HAZELNUT CHOCOCHIP COOKIES
BALLOON
&WHISK
penelope
PINEAPPLE TART COOKIES
BALLOON
&WHISK
FINN
GULA JAWA SABLE COOKIES
BALLOON
&WHISK
LUNA
RED VELVET COOKIES
LOLA
VANILLA BUTTERSCOTCH COOKIES
BALLOON
&WHISK

NÓŻ

Design Agency • **Fajne Chlopaki**
Art Direction • **Fajne Chlopaki**
Illustration • **Łukasz Zbieranowski**
Photography • **Jacek Jakubowski**

NÓŻ is a Spanish restaurant based in Lodz, Poland. Inspired by the name of the restaurant, which means "knife" in Polish, Fajne Chlopaki created the identity of NÓŻ by using geometry to show the concept—everything sharp, as if cut by a knife.

LOGO

NÕŻ
COMIDA Y BEBIDA

FONT · Gotham

ABCDEFGHIJKLM
NOPQRSTUVWXYZ
abcdefghijklm
nopqrstuvwxyz
1234567890

COLOR

C0 M90 Y100 K0
C0 M40 Y100 K0
C100 M80 Y10 K0
C100 M20 Y100 K0

GRAPHIC

NÕZ
COMIDA Y BEBIDA
DANIA GŁÓWNE / MAINS
do de frijoles
ternera

NÕZ
COMIDA Y BEBIDA

NÕZ
COMIDA Y BEBIDA

NÕZ

NÕZ
CERVEZA

NÕÑZ
COMIDA Y BEBIDA

Hardy: Smoked Masterpieces

Design Agency • **This is Pacifica**
Creative Direction • **This is Pacifica**
Client • **Hardy**
Photography • **Nuno Moreira**

Hardy is a heritage of time with a contemporary flavor—smoked salmon according to a German smoke formula and Portuguese knowledge. Hardy's graphic identity results from two main ideas: the use and manipulation of a strong typography that evokes a Germanic aesthetic—rigid and sharp as a cutting knife—and the symbol that reproduces the Hardy process, the salmon fillet, with its texture and repetition of pattern, and a drawstring tie that binds it to the smoker. The visual representation of the fish is adapted to other fishes in the Hardy portfolio. The chromatic palette was defined with great care: The salmon orange and a deep blue exist in balance and in alternation.

LOGO

HARDY
SMOKED MASTERPIECES

FONT • Custom Font

HARDY

COLOR

C0 M73 Y91 K0

GRAPHIC

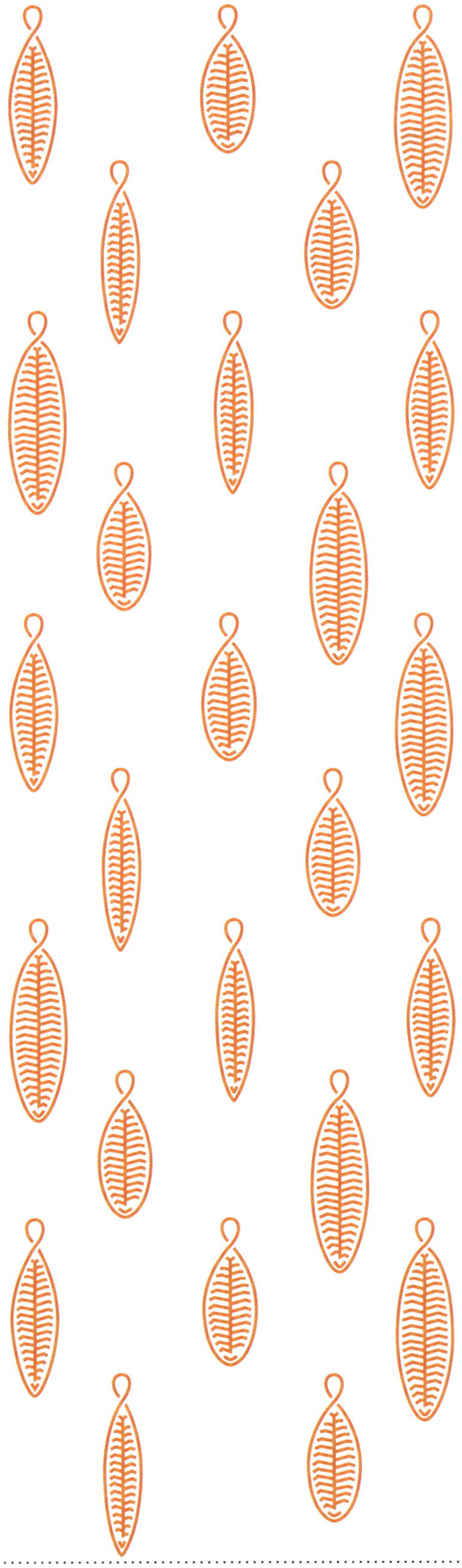

HARDY
SMOKED
MASTERPIECES

HARDY
SMOKED MASTERPIECES
SALMON

HARDY
SMOKED MASTERPIECES
SALMON

SALMON
LACHS

HARDY
SMOKED MASTERPIECES
SALMON

HARDY
SMOKED
MASTERPIECES

HARDY

Ströck

Design Agency • **Bleed**
Art Direction • **Astrid Feldner, Bleed**
Design • **Marc Damm**
Client • **Ströck Brot**
Photography • **Paul Bauer**

Ströck is one of Austria's biggest and oldest bakery brands, a family business that runs over seventy shops in Vienna. The task of Bleed was brand refreshment without changing core elements, such as the logo or the yellow brand color. In order to rejuvenate Ströck's identity, Bleed developed a graphics system which was applied to a coherent packaging line, signage, and point-of-sale implementations. High-quality ingredients, handmade tradition, and a sustainable production process are Ströck's core values. Using these aspects as key hints resulted in a series of grain patterns and various illustrations to enrich the world of Ströck, making it accessible, friendly and more humane.

LOGO

FONT · MaisonNeue

ABCDEFGHIJKLM
NOPQRSTUVWXYZ
abcdefghijklm
nopqrstuvwxyz
1234567890

COLOR

C0 M10 Y100 K0
C12 M22 Y35 K12
C0 M2 Y5 K8
C40 M50 Y60 K45

GRAPHIC

Ströck
stroeck.at

Ströck

UNSERE SÜSSE SEITE
Apfelstrudel 3,70
mit Schlagobers oder Vanillesoße, warm serviert
Topfenstrudel 3,70
mit Schlagobers oder Vanillesoße, warm serviert
Ströcks Pancakes 3,70
mit hausgemachtem Beerenjoghurt (auf Wunsch mit Ahornsirup)
Ströcks Joghurt-Rexglas 3,70
mit frischen Früchten, Müsli, Walnüssen, Chiasamen,
Honig & frischem Fruchtpüree
Kleines Joghurt im Glas 3,70
mit frischem Fruchtpüree
sweet!
Unsere Mitarbeiter informieren Sie gerne über allergene Zutaten in unserem Angebot.
12
VORMITTAG
bio
mhhh

PIKANTE PARADEISER
KÜRBIS MANGO

HAND,
HERZ,
HIRN
Unvergleichliche Qualität, Liebe zum Handewerk und das
Wissen um die besten Zutaten macht unser Brot einfach gut.
Ströck
stroeck.at

Groomery

Design Agency • **Design Studio B.O.B.**

Groomery is a cosmetic brand for men that supplies products for beards. The illustrations are broken down to their essence and communicate their message due to minimal but still characteristic outline drawings. The wordmark itself has been "shaved," showing cutouts in its typography, which makes it a highly recognizable and characteristic logo. Hatchings and full-color areas point out accents and help to explain the handling of the tools and products. All of these elements form the identity of Groomery, which reinvented the shaving process for young and sophisticated men.

LOGO

GROOMERY
THE BARBER´S CHOICE

FONT • FranklinGothicURW

ABCDEFGHIJKLM
NOPQRSTUVWXYZ
abcdefghijklm
nopqrstuvwxyz
1234567890

COLOR

C79 M57 Y49 K44   C10 M11 Y75 K0

GRAPHIC

GROOMERY
THE BARBER'S CHOICE

GROOMERY
THE BARBER'S CHOICE

BALTIC KITCHEN

Design Agency ● **Founded**

BALTIC Kitchen is a reinvention of the original BALTIC Café, a popular destination on the quayside in Gateshead, UK, placing a new focus on its food offerings. Founded created a playful identity around a new set of kitchen icons, drawn to match the roughened character of the unique BALTIC Affisch typeface.

LOGO

BALTIC KITCHEN

FONT · BALTIC Affisch

BALTIC

COLOR

C0 M0 Y0 K100

GRAPHIC

BALTIC
KITCHEN

BALTIC
KITCHEN

Lava Kitchen

Design • **Isabelle Lin**

Lava Kitchen is a Chinese-food kitchen based in New York City. The client wants to bring truly authentic Chinese cuisine to the United States. The kitchen offers Sichuan food, which is famous for its spiciness. The design required an accent color along with a pattern. The red of the lava represents the hot and spicy nature of the cuisine, a sense of passion, as well as Chinese culture itself. Isabelle Lin also designed a simplified lava graphic for a strong visual identity by using vermilion, complemented by medium blue.

LOGO

LAVA KITCHEN
岩漿 食堂

FONT · A-OTF MaruFoPro

ABCDEFGHIJKLM
NOPQRSTUVWXYZ
abcdefghijklm
nopqrstuvwxyz
1234567890

COLOR

C100 M95 Y5 K0

C14 M90 Y87 K0

GRAPHIC

LAVA KITCHEN
岩漿 食堂

Melt your tongue
LAVA KITCHEN
岩漿 食堂
EST 2016

Science House

Art Direction • **Khazieva Zarina**
Design • **Khazieva Zarina**
Photography • **Khazieva Zarina**

Science House is a camp located outside town, and most of the experiments and classes are held on specially equipped sites in nature. The concept of the camp is to promote science, to make it interesting and useful and to help children to make new discoveries. Khazieva Zarina created a corporate character—the Science House—which became part of the logo and corporate identity. This hero inspires confidence and helps children to orient themselves in a large camp space. In branding, Khazieva Zarina also used patterns that embody the four disciplines of the camp: physics, chemistry, biology, ecology.

LOGO

FONT · Futura

ABCDEFGHIJKLM
NOPQRSTUVWXYZ
abcdefghijklm
nopqrstuvwxyz
1234567890

COLOR

C88 M64 Y1 K0
C100 M96 Y44 K3
C46 M100 Y100 K16
C5 M9 Y44 K0

GRAPHIC

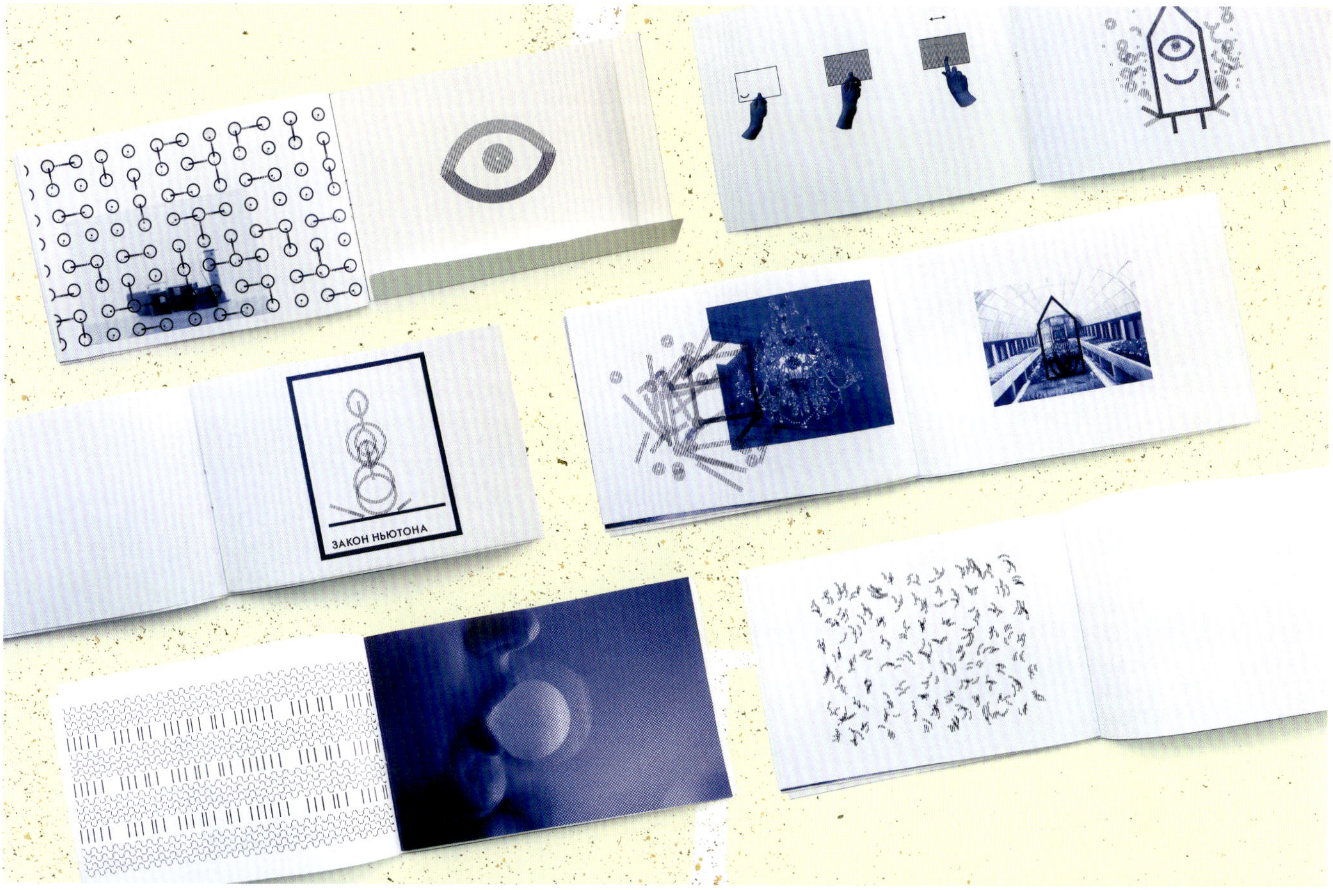
ЗАКОН НЬЮТОНА

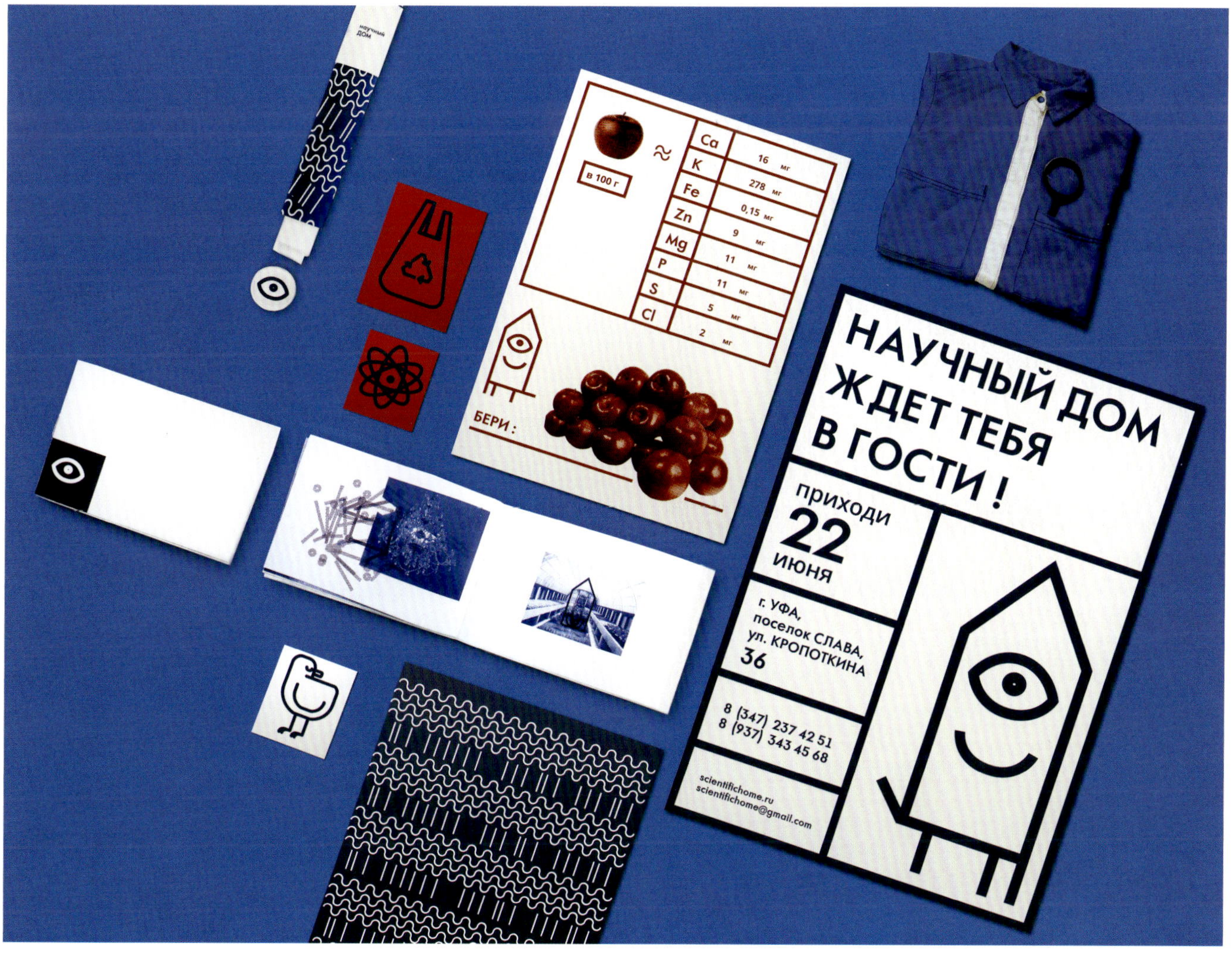
научный
дом
в 100 г
Ca
K
Fe
Zn
Mg
P
S
Cl
16 мг
278 мг
0,15 мг
9 мг
11 мг
11 мг
5 мг
2 мг
БЕРИ :
НАУЧНЫЙ ДОМ
ЖДЕТ ТЕБЯ
В ГОСТИ !
приходи
22
июня
г. УФА,
поселок СЛАВА,
ул. КРОПОТКИНА
36
8 (347) 237 42 51
8 (937) 343 45 68
scientifichome.ru
scientifichome@gmail.com

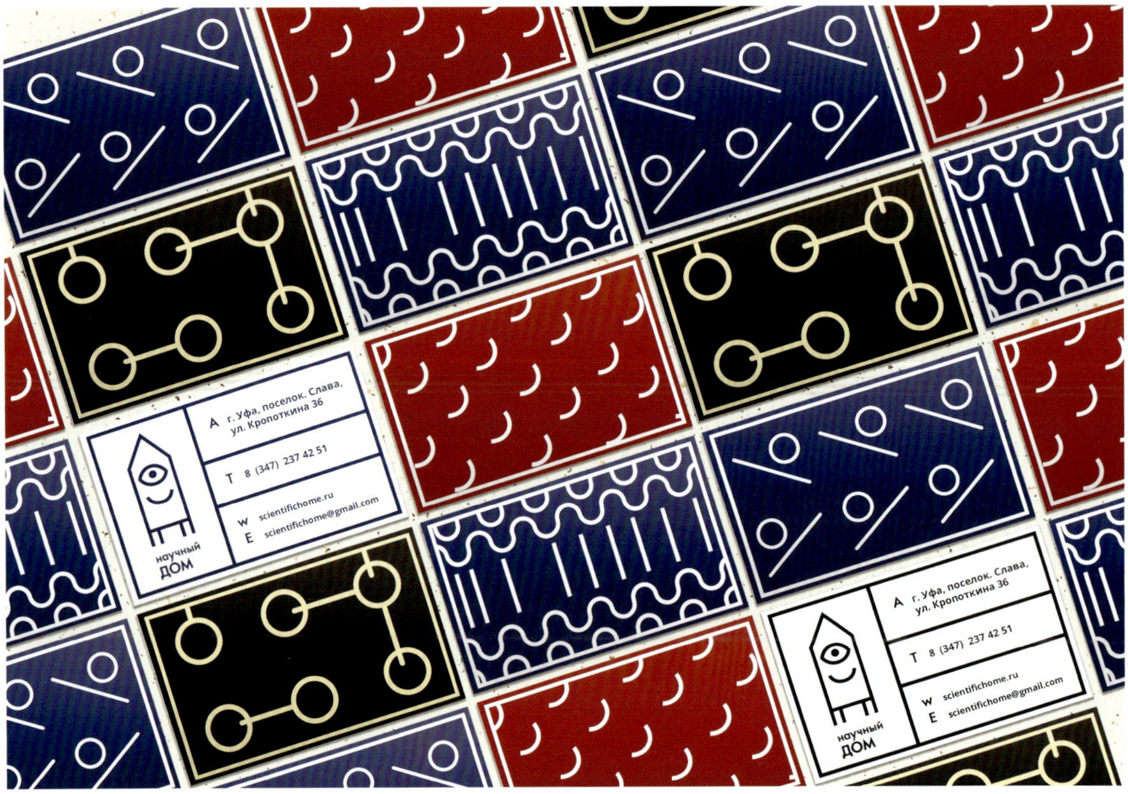
A г. Уфа, поселок. Слава,
ул. Кропоткина 36
T 8 (347) 237 42 51
W scientifichome.ru
E scientifichome@gmail.com
научный
ДОМ

научный
ДОМ
г. Уфа, поселок. Слава,
ул. Кропоткина 36
450056
8 (347) 237 42 51
scientifichome.ru
scientifichome@gmail.com

соблюдайте
меры безопасности

НАУЧНЫЙ ДОМ
ЖДЕТ ТЕБЯ
В ГОСТИ !
приходи
22
июня
г. УФА,
поселок СЛАВА,
ул. КРОПОТКИНА
36
8 (347) 237 42 51
8 (937) 343 45 68
scientifichome.ru
scientifichome@gmail.com

That's Toast

Design • Kinda Ghannoum
Photography • Kinda Ghannoum

That's Toast is an affordable brunch restaurant in Bruges with a culinary identity that revolves around the toast that they serve with every meal. Identity design, packaging, and illustrations on the restaurant walls feature travel imagery, presented with the aesthetic of rubber stamps, following the client's brief. The result is that a young, cosmopolitan and distinctive identity was created.

LOGO

FONT • Asparagus Sprouts

ABCDEFGHIJKLM
NOPQRSTUVWXYZ
abcdefghijklm
nopqrstuvwxyz
1234567890

COLOR

C0 M0 Y0 K0

C0 M0 Y0 K100

GRAPHIC

THAT'S TOAST
All Day Breakfast | Toast Bar

THAT'S
TOAS
All Day B
MENU
HOT DRINKS
Coffee
Ristretto
Espresso
Doppio
Lungo
Americano
Espresso macchiato
Latte macchiato
Flat white
Cappuccino
Latte
Babyccino
Hot chocolate
Tea
Darjeeling
Earl grey
Chinese green tea
Infusion
SOFT STUFF
Homemade lemonade
Homemade ice-tea
Coke, Fanta, Sprite, Tonic, Ginger beer, Bitter lemon
LESS SOFT STUFF
SWEET TOAST
The Triple French €7.5
Toast soaked in milk, eggs, cinnamon and vanilla baked to perfection topped with Nutella pretzels and bacon crumble
Banana boat €6
Peanut butter spread with sliced banana, honey and home-made granola
The Pudding €6.5
Cranberry and pecan bread pudding with cream
SAVORY TOAST
The Classic €8
Avocado salsa, poached egg, green asparagus topped with Grana padano and mint.
The Smashed Pumpkins €7.5
Pumpkin spread, creamy Burrata with crispy parsley and kale.
The Smokey €10.5
Smoked salmon, horseradish cream, Spanish capers, lemon and avocado.
WORLD AROUND
Gotta catch 'm all €12.5
Poke bowl with whole grain rice, marinated salmon, avocado, wakame and pickled ginger.
Toasted dumplings €9
Nuff said
Side salad
Greens and co

Hey!
what's toastin today!

WELCOME

HERE

Dough & Oil

Design Agency • Ico Design

Ico Design created a name and visual identity to brand Shrewsbury's first urban dining experience. They designed an unapologetically bold visual aesthetic that combined expressive typography, a playful tone of voice and a series of playful characters illustrated by Joe Baglow. Collectively these were hand-painted and fly-posted to the exterior and within the restaurant and applied to menus, wine and beer labels, the website, and social media. The result is a playful and modern brand that perfectly fits the mood, food, and service.

LOGO

DOUGH & OIL

FONT • PDU and Prestige

ABCDEabcde
0123456789
ABCDEabcde
0123456789

COLOR

C0 M20 Y10 K0

C0 M95 Y90 K0

C0 M0 Y0 K0

C0 M0 Y0 K100

GRAPHIC

DOUGH & OIL
MADE BY: AARON
FOR: JADE

THIS IS HOW WE DOUGH IT
OIL YEAR ROUND

Lab 180 Gastronomy

Design Agency • **Andstudio**
Art Direction • **Domas Miksys, Augustinas Paukste**
Design • **Domas Miksys, Augustinas Paukste**
Photography • **Martyna Jovaisaite**

Lab 180 is a restaurant located in a converted industrial laboratory in Vilnius, Lithuania, on Street No.180. Andstudio designed the concept, name, and identity, as well as the whole interior. The visual identity was built on the concept of antique illustrations from biology books combined with astronomy and chemistry graphics.

LOGO

LAB 180

FONT • FF Tisa

ABCDEFGHIJKLMN
OPQRSTUVWXYZ
abcdefghijklmnopqrs
tuvwxyz
1234567890

COLOR

C0 M0 Y0 K100

GRAPHIC

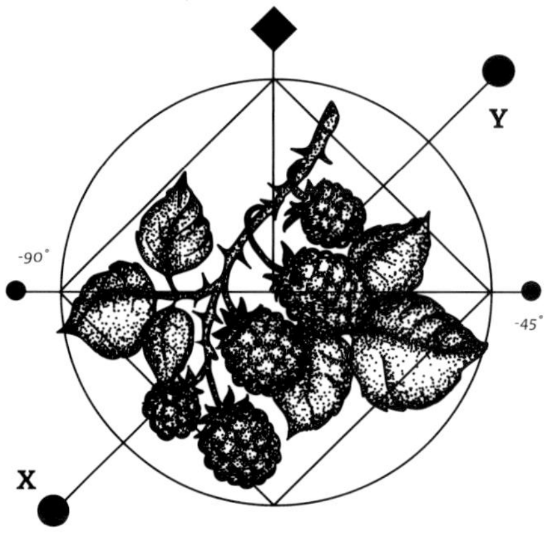

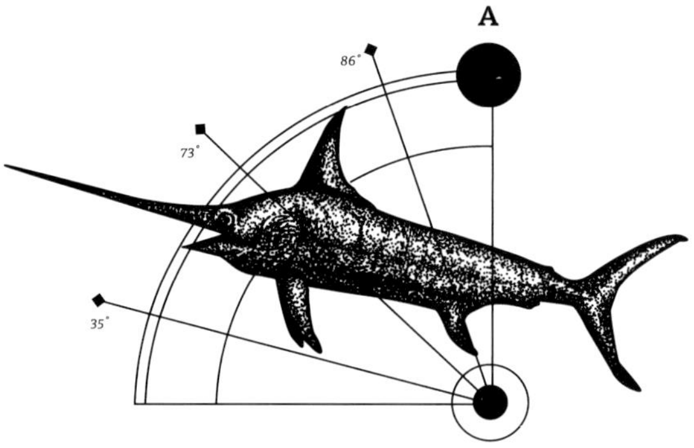

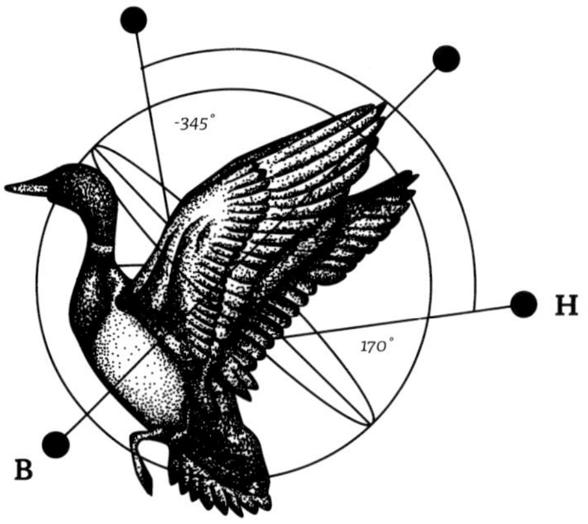

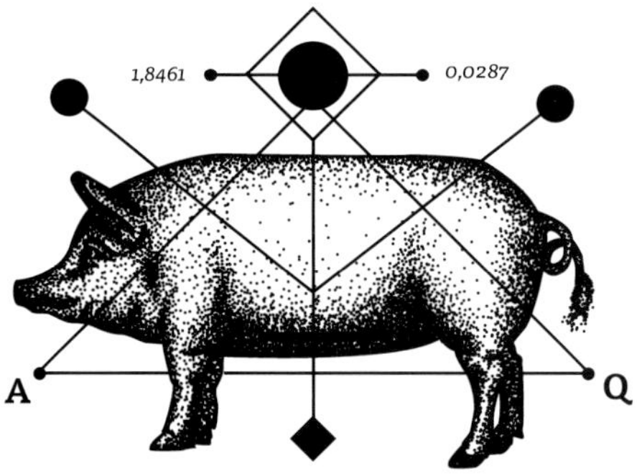

LAB
Price

LAB
Vodka
Price
Skyy 3
Beluga 5
Whiskey
Knob`s Creek RyE bourbon 5
Knob`s Creek 9yo bourbon 5
Bulleit bourbon 3.5
Ledaig 6
Nikka from the barrel 6
Ballantines 4
Rum
Premium white reserva 4
Angostura 5yo 5
Cognac
Hennessy V.S 5.5
Hennessy V.S.O.P 7
330 ml Bottled beer Price
330 ml Cocktails Price

Grüner Michel

Design Agency • **ADDA Studio, Agency Hochburg**

Grüner Michel is a vegetarian restaurant located in Leonberg, in southern Germany. Beyond its food, the restaurant delights the senses—the playful corporate design reveals itself from the logo to the menu, and the trendy but cozy interior design carries ADDA Studio's handwriting.

LOGO

grüner
michel

FONT • Custom Font

der Apfel
fällt nicht
weit vom
stamm

COLOR

C22 M3 Y0 K0

C70 M78 Y62 K28

GRAPHIC

WWW.GRUENER-MICHEL.DE
den Mutigen gehört die Welt
wer zuerst kommt genießt zuerst
der Apfel fällt nicht weit vom Stamm

speis und trank

grüner Michel
grüner Michel
Sehr geehrte Damen und Herren

PEI-TA-HSIANG TEA

Design Agency • **nomo creative**
Art Direction • **Yu Chien Lin**
Design • **Yu Chien Lin, Chi Tai Lin, Wun Siang Huang**
Client • **PEI-TI-HSIANG Culture CO., LTD.**
Calligraphy • **Lin Yen**

Pei-Ti-Hsiang is dedicated to promoting the culture of Taiwanese tea, following Taiwan's professional tea-making artisans. For each tea area with different planting styles and tasting flavors, nomo creative translated the representative elements into abstract visual features. With ink paintings, geometric shapes, and the stylish and modern calligraphy from Taiwanese calligrapher Lin Yen, the identity conveys the refined yet simple charm of the tea ceremony. Nomo creative used colored paper with a strong Asian style and wool paper with a rough surface in the packaging to simulate the texture of an ancient Chinese handmade book. The package design combines modern design with classic concepts, depicting cultural atmosphere and philosophical beauty for Pei-Ti-Hsiang.

LOGO

FONT · Garamond

ABCDEFGHIJKLM
NOPQRSTUVWXYZ
abcdefghijklm
nopqrstuvwxyz
1234567890

COLOR

C80 M57 Y77 K20
C95 M72 Y56 K20
C33 M19 Y47 K0
C44 M17 Y28 K0

GRAPHIC

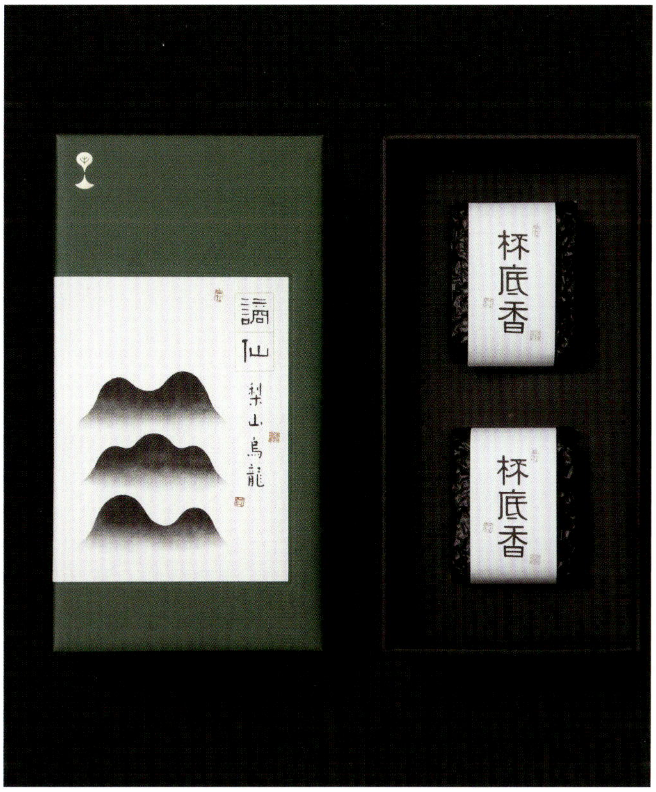
謫仙
梨山烏龍
杯底香
杯底香

獨寬
碳焙烏龍
落英繽紛
東方美人
芳雅
文山包種

Il Balzo

Design Agency • **Lander Project**
Art Direction • **Lander Project**
Client • **Il Balzo**
Photography • **Davide Bischeri**

The wine produced by Il Balzo winery, in the Rufina area, is a merger of two souls. A strong and rough woodcutter meets a passionate and experimental winemaker. Wood and wine, two living materials strictly bound to one another, integrated through perfect osmosis. Lander Project created an identity with wood grain which reveals the merger of the two souls.

LOGO

IL BALZO

FONT • AkzidenzGroteskBE

ABCDEFGHIJKLM
NOPQRSTUVWXYZ
abcdefghijklm
nopqrstuvwxyz
1234567890

COLOR

C0 M0 Y0 K100

C54 M11 Y0 K0

GRAPHIC

L'UOMO
L'AZIENDA
NEL CUORE DEL CHIANTI RUFINA
3ha
OLIVETI
5ha
VIGNETI
IL BALZO
22ha
PASCOLO
SEMINATIVO
BOSCO
TITOLARE PODERE IL BALZO
OGGI SUI 30 ETTARI DELL'AZIENDA
ADDIACCIO
DUEMILA15
UNA SCOMMESSA VINTA CONTRO IL TEMPO,
15
14% vol.
TOSCANA IGT
2015
ADDIACCIO NASCE NEL SETTEMBRE DEL 2015,
NELLA BOTTE AVVIENE IL MIRACOLO:
PAOLO PONTICELLI
www.podereilbalzo.it

IL BALZO
TOSCANA IGT
ALTO
IL BALZO
15
ADDIACCIO
TOSCANA IGT
14% VOL.

IL BALZO
15
ADDIACCIO

INDEX

Asya Demidova

www.behance.net/asya_demidova

Asya Demidova is an art director and graphic designer based in Moscow, currently living in Dublin. She focuses on creating conceptual solutions which provide engaging experiences. In her projects she loves to combine digital and physical space, including illustration and set design, implementing new technologies and different mediums.

P014–015

Anthony Lam

www.behance.net/anthonycheukwang

Anthony Lam is a multidisciplinary designer specializing in visual identity, branding, illustration, and editorial design.

P044–045

Aurėja Jucevičiūtė

www.behance.net/AukseMari

Aurėja Jucevičiūtė is a graphic designer and freelance artist based in Lithuania.

P062–063

A Work of Substance

www.aworkofsubstance.com

Substance is a collective of people with imaginations so far-reaching that if they were a single hybrid person you would probably be afraid to be their friend. Their productivity is not purely achieved by sitting at the desk. Napping for the explicit reason of conjuring surreal ideas is completely justifiable.

P112–115

Anton Skalkin

www.behance.net/skalkinanton

Anton Skalkin is a graphic and web designer based in Russia.

P170–171

Aleksandra Lampart

www.behance.net/Lampart

Aleksandra Lampart is a graphic designer based in Poland.

P178–179

Andstudio

www.andstudio.lt

Andstudio is a branding studio specializing in strategy, visual identities and communication design. They design with purpose and meaning, connecting businesses and audiences for brands to make them become more thrilling and long-lasting.

P224–225

ADDA Studio

www.adda-studio.de

ADDA is a studio for analog and digital media. On a conceptual basis, they develop projects in the areas of corporate design, communication, and digital media. Their customers are located in a wide variety of industries. They work independently of any industry, which is their challenge and their clients' advantage. Quality and a distinctive profile ensure recognition. That is why they believe that it is important to focus on individuality. They develop concepts that have an independent character and reflect their clients' unique selling points.

P226–227

Bruch—Idee & Form

www.studiobruch.com

Bruch—Idee & Form is a nationally and internationally awarded design studio based in Graz. They develop visual design concepts and appropriate strategies for the fields of branding, editorial design, packaging and signage. They strive for flexible solutions, new approaches, differentiation and authenticity.

P030–031

Basic Studio

www.basic.lat

Basic is a design studio that develops creative brands. They communicate the value of the brand through design. Their philosophy leads to an individual scheme development for every client. They keep in mind that essential principles of design help them to amplify unique assets and assist them to build an outstanding brand in the market.

P174–175

Bleed

www.bleed.com

Bleed is an independent design consultancy with offices in Oslo and Vienna. With a unique mix of competencies, they help their clients create outstanding experiences and identities.

P204–207

Charlotte Got

www.behance.net/charlottegot

Charlotte Got is a web and graphic designer with more than eight years of experience. She helps businesses to communicate and promote their activity by creating user interfaces, visuals, and illustrations.

P070–073

Diferente

www.diferente.info

Devoted to creating thriving brands, Diferente helps people to reveal the differential value of their business idea through analytical research, strategic insight and clever design.

P022–023

DekoRatio Branding & Design Studio

www.dekoratio.hu/design/en

DekoRatio is a dedicated design agency that specializes in empowering ambitious businesses through original design. They create beautiful, strong and consistent visual identities through conceptual logo design, illustration, and typography.

P036–037

Dorogobogato Design Bureau

www.dorogobogato.design

Dorogobogato Design Bureau is an independent community of Russian designers who generate ideas and designs, create brands, draw illustrations, and develop names and advertising concepts.

P148–151

Design Studio B.O.B.

www.behance.net/designstudiobob

Studio B.O.B. is a studio for design, branding, and photography, founded by Lilly Friedeberg, Alessia Sistori, and Marc Oortman.

P208–209

Estudio Altillo

Estudioaltillo.com

Estudio Altillo is a multi-disciplinary workspace that finds graphic, branding and communication solutions to its clients' everyday challenges. They are driven by the quest to beautify the way businesses operate, be they small startups or global multinationals. And they go about it by engaging clients throughout their creative process.

P052–055

Estudio Yeyé

Yeye.design

Estudio Yeyé specializes in graphic design, photography, publicity and illustration. Their principal goal is simple: To give their clients work that is relevant, innovative and of the utmost quality.

P094–097, P098–099

Estudio Nuar

www.estudionuar.com

Estudio Nuar is a creative studio specializing in branding. Based in Buenos Aires, they create and strengthen brands throughout the country.

P100–103

Emma Lucia Newnes

emmalucia.net

Emma Lucia Newnes is a graphic designer based in Australia.

P162–165

Fajne Chlopaki

www.fajnechlopaki.com

Fajne Chlopaki is a graphic design studio specializing in the design of book covers and the visual identification of brands from the business and culture sectors. In design, they are guided by honesty and reliability which translates into the fact that they always want to get to know the client, context, needs, and resources to promote them with a clear conscience and not to mislead the recipient. That's why they do not cooperate with everyone.

P160–161, P184–185, P196–199

Founded

Founded.design

Founded is a UK-based design consultancy. They create original, effective and long-lasting solutions for commercial and cultural clients by offering a collaborative and uncomplicated creative process.

P210–211

GM Creative Studio

www.behance.net/gaomuoicreative

GM is "Rice & Salt." The simple name with the desire is also simple. GM wants to do what is strong, favorite and deep. From there, they have the food which means rice and the aftertaste which means salt through each product they make. GM stands for "Rice-Salt," the Vietnamese language hoping to make ends meet and bring their hearts and soul through their products.

P038–041

Gilian Gomes

www.behance.net/giliangomes

Gilian Gomes is a graphic designer based in Brazil.

P142–145

Hue Studio

www.huestudio.com.au

Hue Studio is a South Melbourne-based design studio with a broad spectrum in design, personality and color.

P130–133, P172–173

Hmmm Creative Studio

hmmmcreative.com

Hmmm Creative Studio is a multi-disciplinary Tallinn-based collective specializing in visual ideas through creativity and culture.

P180–181

H3l Branding Agency

www.h3lweb.com

H3l Branding Agency was born in 2004 in Argentinian Patagonia. It is an independent studio that stands out for innovative ideas and creative work. Their team develops commercial and art projects of global significance.

P188–191

ICARUS

www.icarus-creative.com

ICARUS creative is an international award-winning agency for communication and design from Innsbruck. Their name is their inspiration. They conceive design without limits, realize solutions, offer creative focus, carry out brand development and brand management at the highest level and create key visuals and branding for brands and all media channels with maximum impact nationally and internationally.

P088–089, P108–111

Isabelle Lin

www.behance.net/linhsi

Isabelle Lin, a graphic designer based in Guangzhou, started the ISA design studio in 2013, specializing in brand identity, logotype, packaging design, etc. She has a great passion for graphic design. The designer herself is a proponent of minimalism, therefore her work conveys similar ideas: clear, simple, meaningful, and unique, but also very powerful.

P212–213

Ico Design

https://icodesign.com

Ico is a London-based design studio that creates and builds memorable brands for businesses and organizations with ambition.

P222–223

Kurppa Hosk

www.kurppahosk.com

Kurppa Hosk is a diverse team of design thinkers and design doers. They collaborate with brave organizations from early-stage startups to some of the world's most admired companies. They use business, brand and experience design to inform and inspire meaningful change. They do this through "business artistry," an approach that combines commercial and behavioral research, insight and analysis with boldness, beauty, technology, and meticulous craftsmanship.

P024–027

KittoKatsu

www.kittokatsu.de

Established in 2015, KittoKatsu is a small agency specializing in brand strategy and design. They work with a broad range of clients from individuals and institutions to local businesses and global brands. They believe in strong brand management as an essential steering instrument for companies. That is why, in each project, they aim to combine brand strategy and design, developing the brand personality together with their clients and then transforming it into a unique visual identity. The name KittoKatsu, derived from a Japanese saying meaning, "You will surely win," expresses not only their love for all things Japanese but also the promise they make to their clients.

P078–081

Kinoto Studio

kinotostudio.com/

Kinoto Studio is a graphic design studio based in Buenos Aires, Argentina.

P176–177

Khazieva Zarina

www.behance.net/kinotostudio

Khazieva Zarina is a designer and illustrator based in Ufa, Russia.

P214–217

Kinda Ghannoum

www.behance.net/kindaghannoum

Kinda Ghannoum is a freelance graphic designer based in Belgium.

P218–221

Luminous Design Group

www.luminous.gr

Luminous Design Group is an Athens-based storytelling studio. Their design services include branding, identity, print, and digital design, packaging design and creative direction. They focus on branding and design with purpose, approaching every project with passion, producing expressive, bold and innovative communication.

P058–059

LIE DESIGN & ART DIRECTION

www.wearenotlie.com

LIE is an acronym for Little Ideas Everyday, an independent graphic design studio based in Kuala Lumpur. Founded in 2011, LIE works across a diverse range of visual communication projects, constantly practicing and seeking fresh approaches every day, providing innovative, beautiful solutions for clients, as well as self-initiated projects. Not sticking to the norm or patterns, they believe there's always room to explore in design.

P118–119, P120–121, P146–147

Lander Project

www.landerproject.it/

Lander Project takes care of different aspects related to brand communication and marketing: Starting from brand identity, packaging, graphic design, logo restyling, and illustration all the way up to advertising and marketing campaigns online and offline.

P230–232

Masha Knop

Mashaknop.com

Masha Knop is a young professional with a Master's degree in graphic design, and she knows what real design is. She knows how to make it and how to spice it. She loves to think and create, contemplate and learn. Each project is a challenge and there is no other way but to be a winner. Her aim is to build a visually pleasing environment, squeezing out non-pros and amateurs.

P032–033

Mubien

mubien.com

Mubien is a design studio specializing in branding and identity design. Mubien helps new businesses and brands get started or revitalizes and revolutionizes existing ones for growth through carefully crafted design and strategic thinking.

P106–107

Menta Picante

www.mentapicante.mx

Menta Picante is a studio of husband and wife from Guadalajara, focused on the development of graphic identities for brands. For them, it is very important to connect with each one of their clients to know the needs of their projects and therefore to develop a brand which speaks for itself and tells its story in a visual way.

P156–157

Makebardo

www.makebardo.com

Makebardo is a creative design studio based in Queenstown, New Zealand. The studio practices contemporary visual communication specializing in brand identities, packaging design and wayfinding systems for national and international clients.

P158–159

MONOTYPO Studio

monotypo.com

MONOTYPO Studio is a business services agency specializing in visual communication and graphic design. Their main objective is to leave a graphic imprint of neatness, simplicity, cleanliness, aesthetics and functionality on each of their products. Also, that each of their customers feels a total satisfaction with their services. They analyze the needs of their clients and offer integral solutions to them, addressing their current situation, their mission and vision, establishing *a posteriori* of these the guidelines to which the project will be directed graphically, its personality and its conceptual structure.

P192–193

Nadja Olić

www.behance.net/NadjaOlic

Nadja Olić is a graphic designer and artist based in Serbia.

P104–105

Necon

necon.co

Necon works with businesses to explore the mysterious underlying communication dynamics and find the right means of future expression. Their goal is to invade a time of change and push it beyond what people expect of it.

P134–135

Nomo Creative

nomocreative.com

Nomo creative is a design studio from Taiwan,China. Founded in 2015, with different experienced people from various backgrounds, the nomo creative showcase covers various industries including fashion, art, catering, entertainment, and technology. They stand for concise, contemporary design with a unique but distinct image. They start a journey without boundaries, engaging with cultures and humanity. Nomo creative explores every inch of a process and believes every piece of achievement has its own scene.

P228–229

Oscar Bastidas

mor8graphic.com

Oscar Bastidas is a freelance graphic designer based in the USA.

P042–043, P046–049, P152–155

Ostecx Créative

www.ostecx.com

Ostecx Créative loves the brands for which they work and hopes it shows. In their work, they blend advertising, promotion, and design. They do not like to be confined within rigid limits. Therefore, their portfolio includes advertising campaigns, sales promotions and increasing numbers of branding and packaging. They all feel good when they have the opportunity to create a brand and introduce it to the market, and they do not want to deny pleasure to themselves or to their customers.

P182–183

Plus X

www.plus-ex.com

Plus X is a brand experience marketing and design partner aiming for the best design output which any business would seek for its brand in diverse media's marketing point to deliver an accurate user experience. Plus X has a connotation of "We Add Experience for Your Brand." Brand experience design means providing consumers with valuable brand experience through consolidated online and offline designs based on the consistent brand strategy. They believe that key brand messages or service functions can be effectively delivered when various media channels meet strategic marketing.

P010–013

Project On Museum

www.projectonmuseum.com

Project On Museum is a design and strategy team from Taiwan, China. Their team members are from different backgrounds such as graphic design, business and marketing. They focus on helping people to build their brands and promoting products through design and storytelling.

P016–019

Pentagram

www.pentagram.com

Pentagram is the world's largest independently-owned design studio. Their work encompasses graphics and identity, architecture and interiors, products and packaging, exhibitions and installations, websites and digital experiences, advertising and communications. They are the only major design studio where the owners of the business are the creators of the work and serve as the primary contact for every client. This reflects their conviction that great design cannot happen without passion, intelligence and above all personal commitment, and is demonstrated by a portfolio that spans five decades and all industries.

P020–021, P126–129

Petr Kudlacek

www.lilkudley.cz

Petr Kudlacek is a graphic designer, art director and occasional illustrator from Prague, Czech Republic. He acquired his work experience during the four years he worked in the multidisciplinary studio Fundaluka. Since 2013 he has been freelancing under the name Lilkudley. He likes most to occupy himself with visual identities, from website wireframe designs to selecting colored paper for business cards. In order to be able to work on these projects, he surrounds himself with competent programmers, motion designers, and photographers.

P028–029

Pauline Pourcelot

be.net/eniluap

Pauline Pourcelot is a graphic designer based in France.

P166–167

Quattrolinee

www.quattrolinee.it

Quattrolinee is a graphic design agency focused on identity creation and brand development. They help startups, companies and public authorities to develop new relationships with people.

P074–077

Simon Piu

www.behance.net/SimonPiu

Simon Piu is a graphic designer and art director based in France.

P056–057

Studio Fnt

www.studiofnt.com

Studio Fnt is a Seoul-based graphic design studio that works on prints, identities, digital media and more. It collects fragmented and straying thoughts and then organizes and transforms them into relevant forms.

P060–061

Serious Studio

www.serious-studio.com

Serious Studio is a design consultancy firm for big and small brands around the world. Their core philosophy is: Make Sense and Look Good. It is really simple. They believe that effective communication happens when strategy and design go hand-in-hand. Aside from being astonishingly smart and being someone you can bring home to your family, the authenticity in what they do makes their work soulfully exceptional. This has made them successful outliers in their respective industries.

P082–085, P168–169

Sorokina Natalia

www.behance.net/natalia_sorokina

Sorokina Natalia is a graphic designer and illustrator based in Russia.

P086–087

Shangning Wang

www.behance.net/Shangning

Shangning Wang is a New York-based award-winning graphic designer, illustrator, and all-around creative. He focuses on branding design, data visualization, commercial art, illustration, report design, website design, and poster design.

P136–137

Stella Shih

www.projectonmuseum.com

Stella Shih is a graphic designer based in Taiwan, China.

P138–141

The Woork Co.

thewoork.co

The Woork Co. is a branding studio based in Spain. Their mission is helping brands to find their image and voice in digital, print and audiovisual media.

P034–035

Tina Homewood

tinahomewood.myportfolio.com

Tina Homewood is an extremely driven graphic designer with a keen interest in branding. After completing work experience in Australia and Indonesia she is looking for a new challenge and an opportunity to grow as a designer. She is committed to self-development and has been developing her skills through self-initiated briefs, online courses, and freelance work.

P068–069

The Goort

thegoort.com

The Goort is a design bureau in Ukraine. They prefer functionality throughout and honest and thoughtful architecture and design.

P090–093

Tyodi Hyojin Lee

www.tyo-stitch.com/Lee-hyo-jin

Tyodi Hyojin Lee is a brand experience designer in Seoul, South Korea. He attempts to deliver the differentiated brand experience by boundlessly agonizing at the various intersections of brand and customers. He makes diverse graphic-and-illustration-based attempts, including branding, based on antique things, new things, experience, and value.

P122–125

Thinking*Room

thinkingroominc.com

Tingking*Room is a design company based in Jakarta, Indonesia, founded in 2005 and known for pushing the limits. They have gained the trust of many of their clients to focus on total designs and concepts solutions. Through their intuitive approach and crafted skills, they have used both traditional and non-traditional methods to communicate the different elements of the brand. They serve full-design-service, focus on brand identities, strategy, campaign, content creation, products and packaging, books, websites, social media, motion, interiors, exhibition, installations, environments, and more.

P194–195

This is Pacifica

www.thisispacifica.com

This is Pacifica is an independent communication studio based in Porto, Portugal, established in 2007. They do branding, graphic design, interactive design, web design, packaging, signs, space design, editorial, motion graphics, mobile design, advertising, events, and relationship marketing.

P200–203

Untitled Macao

www.behance.net/untitledmacao

Untitled Macao, founded by a young Macao designer, Au Chon Hin, is a design studio which specializes in graphic design for event images, brand identities, publications, websites, and apps.

P050–051

We are two

wearetwo.gr

We are two is a graphic design studio based in Xanthi, Greece. Their job is to visualize, every time, what the customer wants to communicate. Every case is unique, and after discussion with the customer, thorough study and personalized design they will suggest comprehensive solutions to visual communication. Their services include brand identity, naming, web design, development, art direction, print design and package design.

P116–117

Xfacta

www.xfacta.co.za

Xfacta is a bespoke strategic design, brand and concept agency. The team prides itself on solid strategic insights and strong client relationships, allowing for quick turnarounds and rigorous brand alignment throughout the client's business. A key differentiator is that they push to think further than the conventional industry norms, and the results are visible in their work. Central to their philosophy is that business success is driven by creative solutions, and that the right questions lead to deep understanding.

P064–067

Yuan Wang

wangyuan.de

Yuan is a graphic designer based in Germany and China who focuses on graphic design, visual identities, illustration, book design and more.

P186–187

ACKNOWLEDGEMENTS

We would like to express our gratitude to all of the designers and companies for their generous contribution of images, ideas, and concepts. We are also very grateful to many other people whose names do not appear in the credits but who made specific contributions and provided support. Without them, the successful compilation of this book would not be possible. Special thanks to all of the contributors for sharing their innovation and creativity with all of our readers around the world.